DIRTY BOXING
FOR MIXED MARTIAL ARTS

MATT LINDLAND

with GLEN CORDOZA & ERICH KRAUSS

LAS VEGAS

First Published in 2009 by Victory Belt Publishing.

ISBN 10: 0-9815044-4-2

ISBN 13: 978-0-9815044-4-5

Cover Design by Michael J. Morales, VIP GEAR

Printed in Hong Kong

Contents

PART ONE: BASIC SKILLS

1.1 SEVEN BASIC SKILLS

1.2 BASIC POSITIONING

1.3 BASIC CONTROLS

1.4 TWO-ON-ONE CONTROL SETUPS

1.5 UNDERHOOK SETUPS

1.6 TRANSITIONING TO CONTROL POSITIONS

PART TWO: TAKEDOWN SETUPS

2.1 TWO-ON-ONE TECHNIQUES (ARM DRAG)

2.2 UNDERHOOK TECHNIQUES

2.3 HEAD CONTROL TECHNIQUES

PART THREE: FINISHING THE TAKEDOWN

3.1 DOUBLE-LEG FINISHES

3.2 SINGLE-LEG FINISHES

3.3 BACK CONTROL FINISHES

PART FOUR: TAKEDOWN DEFENSE

4.1 TAKEDOWN DEFENSE 101

4.2 DOUBLE-LEG DEFENSE

4.3 SINGLE-LEG DEFENSE

PART FIVE: STRIKING

ABOUT THIS BOOK

Three years prior to winning the Greco-Roman Silver Metal in the 2000 Olympic Games, I stepped into the cage for the first time to test my hand at mixed martial arts competition. The sport was still in its infancy, and so was my fighting style. I had little experience in either striking or the art of submission. I came armed solely with the techniques I had acquired from a lifetime of wrestling. With the majority of competitors still not having realized the importance of cross-training in a number of martial arts disciplines, I was able to dominate. I'd take my opponent to the mat, control him on the ground, and then pound him into submission with rudimentary strikes. Although this tactic worked well for me right out of the gates, I watched as the sport slowly started to evolve. As more and more fighters learned how to defend against takedowns and neutralize ground-and-pound assaults, I saw the need to evolve as well. Going back to the drawing board, I began developing a system of fighting that would allow me to use my wrestling effectively against the new breed of cross-trained fighters.

I began studying boxing and submission wrestling, but the goal was not to become a master boxer or jiu-jitsu phenom because it would require me to steer away from my strong wrestling base. The entire mission with picking up these new forms of fighting was to make my wrestling more effective. I learned how to use my newly acquired strikes and submissions to set up wrestling techniques, and I developed ways to use my wrestling techniques to set up strikes and submissions. Although my fighting skills improved dramatically with this new combination, there were still some bumps in the road. A lot of the wrestling moves that I had been using effectively on the mats for years can leave a fighter vulnerable to strikes and submissions when fighting in the cage. Not wanting to get knocked out or choked unconscious, I began weeding out the wrestling techniques that didn't translate well to MMA. The process of building this new style took many years, but the end result was a highly effective wrestling-based form of fighting. This is the system that I teach to my students, many of whom are now competing at the top tier of MMA competition, and it is the system I offer in this book.

The first sections are designed to provide you with a strong wrestling base. Even if you have a background in wrestling, I strongly recommend reviewing the opening chapters because without a sturdy foundation of proper movement and fundamental techniques, the attacks presented in later chapters will not only be difficult to understand, but also nearly impossible to pull off effectively. As you will see, I emphasize the importance of setups and transitions. Understanding the movements involved in these techniques is only a minor part of the battle—to truly become a master at setups and transitions you must practice them tirelessly in the gym to acquire the proper timing and sense of distance.

It is important to note that this manual only covers the stand-up portion of my system, which includes standing control positions, striking, off-balancing techniques, takedowns, throws, takedown defense, and the dirty boxing clinch. With all MMA fights starting in the stand-up position, it is important to master this realm of combat before tackling the ground game, which will be the focus of my next book. To get the most out of this manual, I strongly recommend working through it sequentially, as each section is a precursor to the one that follows. Once you understand the flow of the system, then and only then should you skip around between the chapters.

The goal of this book is not to teach you every possible technique that you can use in a fight, but rather to teach the system of fighting that I have developed over my lifetime. The techniques that you'll find over the coming pages are the ones that I have used to defeat top MMA fighters in competitions around the world, including the Ultimate Fighting Championship. Although certain techniques might not be suitable to the style you have developed, as long as you keep an open mind, you will learn new techniques and strategies that can take your game to the next level. Train hard, and good luck!

PART ONE: BASIC SKILLS

OVERVIEW

The vast majority of this book is devoted to dynamic attacks such as takedowns and throws from the clinch, but in order to successfully pull off these types of maneuvers, you must first master the basic skills presented in this section. They will be used time and again with both offensive and defensive techniques, and if you choose to skip over them due to their simplistic nature, your entire game will suffer. For the best results, view the coming techniques as the foundation the rest of the book is built upon and train them accordingly.

THE SEVEN BASIC SKILLS (p. 13-21)

The first day a new student comes to my gym, I teach him the seven basic skills, which include stance, motion, elevation change, penetration, the back step, the lift, and the hip heist. In virtually every technique offered in later chapters, one or more of these skills are a critical component of the technique. Without a firm understanding of each skill, you will have a very difficult time employing the attacks presented in this book.

BASIC POSITIONING (p. 24-25)

Whether you are wrestling on the mats or fighting in a cage, attacking your opponent straight on is a recipe for failure. In order to launch an effective attack, you must become a master at creating angles. In this section, I discuss the importance of acquiring a dominant angle, demonstrate how to use a dominant angle to tie your opponent up in the clinch, and then offer instruction on where and how to place your head to secure a dominant clinch control position, which in turn allows you to execute the attacks presented later in the book. Failing to learn these key concepts will make it very difficult to acquire the positioning needed to effectively employ your offense.

BASIC CONTROL POSITIONS (p. 26-28)

In this section I cover three dominant control positions that can be employed while in the clinch—two-on-one control, underhook control, and head control. When you establish any of these positions, you not only dramatically increase your offensive options, but you also rob your opponent of his offensive options. In order for him to attack, he must first clear your control. As you will learn in later chapters, your opponent's escape route from each of these control positions creates openings that can be exploited. However, in the beginning it is important to focus on securing each control position properly. If you fail to lock in a solid hold and threaten your opponent, you dramatically limit your primary attacks. Your opponent also won't feel the need to mount a desperate escape, which limits many of your transitions and secondary attacks. In addition to demonstrating how to secure each of these control positions, I also introduce you to the concept of inside positioning. Although it is not a form of control, it plays a critical roll in the clinching techniques presented later in the book.

TWO-ON-ONE SETUPS (p. 30-36)

In this section I take you one step deeper into two-on-one control by demonstrating multiple ways to set up the position. Whether you are squared off with your opponent in your wrestling stance or tied up with him in the clinch, the first step is to establish a grip on one of his arms. Depending upon the situation, you can use a near grip, cross grip, or inverted grip, all of which are covered. The next step is to establish a second grip on the same arm using your opposite hand. Accomplishing this allows you to control one of your opponent's arms using both of your hands, hence the name two-on-one control. The goal is to use this control to pull your opponent off balance and break his stance. Before he can recover his base, you move your body into the two-on-one control position. I strongly recommend spending a good deal of time practicing the setups covered in this section and the ones to follow. If your setups are weak, you will have a very

hard time reaching one of the dominant control positions. And if you can't establish a dominant control position, the attacks demonstrated later in the book won't be available.

UNDERHOOK SETUPS (p. 38-44)

In order to establish underhook control, you must get inside positioning on your opponent and close the distance between your bodies. Although this sounds rather simple, it can be quite difficult. It requires some trickery. To introduce you to the art of deception, I demonstrate how to set up underhook control using the push/pull method of attack. It's a fairly simple concept—if you push into your opponent, his natural reaction will be to push back, and if you pull on your opponent, his natural reaction will be to pull away. Using certain movements to invoke involuntary reactions out of your opponent is key for setting up the underhook, as well as many of the attacks laid out in this book. However, the window of opportunity cre-

in this section I demonstrate how to flow from one control position to the next based upon your opponent's chosen method of escape. All the control positions covered in this book are interconnected, and as long as you base your transitions on your opponent's movements, you can remain in control of the fight at all times. For example, if your opponent attempts to escape two-on-one control by backing away, you can transition to underhook control on his opposite side or pull his head down and transition to head control. The key is to always remain on the offensive, but to never try to force a particular control position. As long as you continually transition to the closest control position, you can remain one step ahead of your opponent.

ated by your opponent's reaction will most likely be extremely small, making it important to not only practice the movements needed to invoke the reaction, but also the movements needed to capitalize on them. If your timing is off, the window will close and you'll be back to square one.

TRANSITIONING TO CONTROL POSITIONS (p. 46-50)

Securing a dominant control position provides you with a slew of offensive options while limiting the offensive options of your opponent. If you're up against an experienced wrestler or fighter, he will realize his vulnerability the instant you gain control of his body and immediately mount an escape. Although it can sometimes be difficult to prevent that escape, your opponent becomes highly vulnerable in the transitional phase, allowing you to use his retreat to secure a takedown, land strikes, or transition to another form of control. Later in the book I demonstrate the takedown and striking options that can be employed, and

1.1 SEVEN BASIC SKILLS

FIRST BASIC SKILL: STANCE

The first basic skill that you must develop is your stance. As mentioned in the introduction, there are three stances—the wrestling stance, the Greco-Roman stance, and the fighting stance. While the fighting stance will most likely be your primary stance, it is important to become familiar with all three because they each play a roll in fighting. For example, if you want to shoot in for a single- or double-leg takedown, you must transition from your fighting stance into a wrestling stance, and when tied up in the clinch, transitioning into a Greco stance can open up an assortment of attack options. Spending time developing your Greco and wrestling stances might seem counterproductive in the beginning, but in the long run it will make your fighting stance a lot more effective.

    With all three stances, there are some basic rules to follow. First, you want to keep your elbows tight to your body and your hands out in front of you. If your elbows flare out to your sides, it creates an opening that your opponent can exploit. For example, a good freestyle wrestler will use this opening to penetrate past your defenses and work for a takedown, and a good Greco-Roman wrestler will use the opening to establish a dominant position, such as two-on-one or underhook control. In addition to this, the effectiveness of your punches will drop dramatically with your elbows away from your body. The second rule with all three stances is to position your head directly over your lead toe and your chest over your lead knee. This will provide you with a sturdy base and allow you to attack or defend on a moment's notice. To give you the specifics of each of these stances, I have broken them down in detail in the sequences below.

WRESTLING STANCE

When fighting from the standing position in freestyle wrestling, the single- and double-leg takedowns are your primary attacks. In order to be most effective with these attacks, both of which are directed at your opponent's legs, you want to assume a low or crouched stance. To accomplish this, lower your elevation by bending at the knees and sinking your hips back. Your shoulders should be square with your opponent, your back straight, your head lined up with your lead toe, and your chest lined up with your lead knee. If you lean too far forward, backward, or to one side or the other, your balance will be compromised, making you vulnerable to attack. To better illustrate these fine nuances, imagine dangling a plum bob off your head and one off your chest. If you're in a proper stance, the one dangling from your head will line up perfectly to your lead toe and the one dangling from your chest will line up perfectly to your lead knee. Anytime either plum bob swings to one side or the other of your lead foot or knee, your balance will be off. Once you've got the positioning of your body perfect, the next step is to elevate your arms and position your hands in front of your body. Your hands are your first line of defense, and they will also be your primary weapons when attacking.

To assume a wrestling stance, I bend my knees and sink my hips back. It is important to notice the positioning of my feet. The toes of my right foot are pointing at my opponent's centerline, and the toes of my left foot are angled toward my left side at a forty-five-degree angle. My shoulders are square with my opponent, my hands are elevated away from my body, and my elbows are tucked tight to my sides. If you flare your elbows away from your body, your opponent can grab your arms and use them as anchors to set up an attack. Also notice how my back is straight, my chest is positioned over my right knee, and my head is positioned over my right foot. From this position, I am poised to attack or defend.

GRECO STANCE

The Greco stance is similar to the wrestling stance in several regards: You want to keep your shoulders square with your opponent, your back straight, your head positioned over your lead toe, your chest positioned over your lead knee, your elbows tucked to your sides, and your hands up and in front of your body. However, instead of dropping your elevation and assuming a low stance, you raise your elevation by straightening your legs and posturing up. The primary reason behind this stance change has to do with the rules of Greco-Roman wrestling. While in freestyle wrestling most of your attacks focus on your opponent's legs, in Greco you're not allowed to attack the legs. You can only attack your opponent's upper body, utilizing throws and body-lock takedowns. By assuming a high stance, you can better control his upper extremities and achieve your goals. Once you feel comfortable moving about while in both a wrestling and high stance, begin experimenting with your fighting stance, which I cover next.

To establish a Greco stance, I straighten my legs and posture up. Notice the similarities between this stance and a wrestling stance: I have a slight bend in my knees, my back is straight, my elbows are tight to my body, my hands are elevated and positioned out in front of me, the toes of my right foot are pointing at my opponent's centerline, the toes of my left foot are pointed to my left at roughly a forty-five-degree angle, my head is over my lead toe, and my chest is positioned over my lead knee. From here, I can effectively attack or defend.

FIGHTING STANCE

As you now know, a wrestling stance is a low stance, which is best suited for attacking your opponent's legs, and a Greco stance is a high stance, which is best suited for attacking your opponent's upper body. In order to assume an effective fighting stance, you need to acquire a position that allows you to accomplish both tasks. If your stance is too low, it will be difficult to execute and defend against strikes. If your stance is too high, it will be difficult to execute or defend against wrestling takedowns such as single and double-legs. As a result, the best fighting stance is somewhere in the middle. Although your elevation will be between a low stance and a high stance, many of the general principles stay the same—keep your chest positioned over your lead knee, keep your head positioned over your lead toe, and keep your back straight. Unlike in the wrestling and Greco stances, it is important to keep your chin to your chest and your hands up by your head to protect yourself from strikes.

To assume a fighting stance, I bend my knees slightly, tuck my chin to my chest, shrug my shoulders, extend my arms slightly away from my body, and position my hands at eye level. Notice how my head is still positioned over the toes of my right foot and my chest is still positioned over my right knee. From this position, I can quickly drop into a low stance to execute or defend against takedowns, and I can also execute and defend against strikes.

SECOND BASIC SKILL: MOTION

The second basic skill you must master is footwork, which is needed to both attack and to defend against your opponent's attacks. To utilize footwork effectively, you must follow two basic rules. The first and most important rule is to never break your stance. It doesn't matter if you're fighting in MMA or competing in a wrestling match—you never want to break your home stance. If you forget this golden rule, your body and limbs will be out of position, leaving you vulnerable to attack. If you should get hit, knocked off balance, or snapped out of position, always return to your home stance. The second rule is to always move the foot closest to the direction that you want to head. If you want to move to your left, step your left foot first and then drag your opposite foot across the mat in order to maintain your stance. If you want to move forward, step your lead foot forward and then make up the distance by dragging your back foot across the mat. Practicing this simple movement is extremely important because it prevents you from crossing your feet, which compromises your balance and breaks your home stance. As long as you follow these two simple rules, you will have a much easier time acquiring dominant angles of attack, allowing you to increase your offensive options while at the same time decreasing your opponent's ability to attack.

THIRD BASIC SKILL: ELEVATION CHANGE

The third basic skill you must develop is elevation change, which is a critical tool for getting past your opponent's hands. For example, when squared off with your opponent in your fighting stance, his hands will most likely be positioned to defend against your strikes. By quickly dropping from your fighting stance down into a wrestling stance, you can shoot in underneath his hands and attack his body. Although learning how to change your elevation is quite easy, the goal is to maintain your stance as you drop, which can take some practice. Once you feel comfortable dropping from a fighting stance into a low stance, begin working on penetrating into your opponent's body, which is the next basic skill.

I'm in a wrestling stance with my right foot forward, and Ian is in a wrestling stance with his left foot forward. Both of us are looking for an opening to attack.

I drop my elevation by bending my knees and sinking my hips toward the mat. Notice that as I execute this drop, I keep my back straight, my chest positioned over my right knee, and my head centered over my right foot. Having utilized proper form, I have positioned my head underneath my opponent's hands, which will allow me to penetrate into his body.

SEVEN BASIC SKILLS

FOURTH BASIC SKILL: PENETRATION

Once you've learned how to properly drop your elevation, the next step is to practice penetrating into your opponent's body to execute a takedown. To accomplish this from a low stance, drive off the mat with your rear foot and step your lead foot forward. Instead of stopping your forward momentum when you come into contact with your opponent, which is a common mistake, drive through his body. This will force him backward and dramatically increase your chances of successfully executing one of the takedowns described later in the book. If you look at the photos in the sequence below, you'll notice that I've chosen to drop my level and shoot in for takedown as my opponent throws a punch. Not only does this allow me to duck his strike, but with his arm extended and his momentum moving forward, it also will be much harder for him to block my shot by sprawling his hips and legs behind him.

I'm squared off with Ian in my fighting stance, searching for an opening to attack.

As Ian throws a right cross at my head, I duck his strike by bending my knees and sinking my hips toward the mat. Notice how I have kept my hands up to protect my face and head. If you drop your hands too early and reach for your opponent's legs, there is a good chance that you'll get kneed in the face.

Before Ian can pull his right arm back into his stance, I penetrate into his body by driving off my left foot and stepping my right foot forward to the outside of his left leg. Once I've closed the distance, I drive my right shoulder into his chest and wrap my hands around the outside of his hips. From here, I have several takedown options, all of which will be covered later in the book.

FIFTH BASIC SKILL: THE BACK STEP

The fifth basic skill that you need to develop for both wrestling and MMA is the back step, which is used for executing throws, such as the shoulder throw, the headlock throw, and the hip toss. With each of these techniques, the back step allows you to circle your hips into your opponent and then lift him off the mat using the rotation of your body. In the first sequence below, I demonstrate the technique without an opponent so you can get a good grasp of the footwork involved. In the second sequence, I demonstrate how to use the back step to set up a throw. Later in the book I will show all the throws that can be executed using the back step, but for now it is important that you focus on mastering the movements. This requires a healthy amount of drilling. When running through the technique with a partner, there are a couple of things you should keep in mind. First, always keep both feet planted on the mat because it allows you to utilize the full power of your hips. If one foot comes off the mat, you only have half the power. Secondly, when rotating, do not line your hips up with your opponent's hips—you want to rotate your hips past his hips. This will pull your opponent onto your back, allowing you to throw him with little effort using one of the techniques detailed later in the book. If you stop short with your rotation, the throw will be much more difficult to accomplish.

SEQUENCE A: BACK STEP FORWARD (INDEPENDENT MOVEMENT)

I'm in my fighting stance.

I slide my left foot forward and to the outside of my right foot. Notice how my knees are bent and I'm up on the ball of my left foot.

Pivoting on both feet, I rotate in a counterclockwise direction and drop my elevation by bending at the knees and sinking my butt toward the mat. Notice how I kept my back straight and my chest positioned directly over my knees as I executed the turn.

Keeping my chin tucked to my chest, I straighten my legs and come up on to the balls of my feet. To set up my imaginary opponent for a throw, I move my head in front of my feet and slightly hunch my back.

SEQUENCE B: BACK STEP SHOULDER THROW SETUP

In an attempt to secure an underhook, Ian reaches his right arm underneath my left arm. Before he can establish a deep hook, I draw my left elbow into my body to trap his right hand.

I grip Ian's right triceps with my left hand.

Keeping Ian's right arm pinned to my chest using my left arm, I rotate my body in a counterclockwise direction and hook my right arm underneath his right armpit.

I cross my left leg behind my right leg and plant the ball of my left foot on the mat.

Keeping Ian's right arm pinned to my chest, I drop my level by bending at the knees, pivot on both feet, and rotate my body in a counterclockwise direction. Notice how by spinning my hips past his hips, I pull his weight forward and load him onto my back.

Having pulled Ian onto my back, I straighten my legs and pull him off the mat. From here, I can finish the throw by continuing to rotate my body and dumping him to the mat. To see how this is done, along with the other techniques that utilize the back step, visit the Throws section of the book.

SIXTH BASIC SKILL: LIFT

Hoisting your opponent into the air and then slamming him to the mat is a trademark wrestling technique, but in order to be effective at it, you must master the lift, which is the sixth basic skill. Executing a proper lift requires two things—positioning and technique. There are several ways to position your body to set up a lift, most of which stem from an over-under bodylock, a double underhook front bodylock, a side bodylock, or a bodylock from back control. However, you can also achieve a lift from the double-leg, high-crotch, or single-leg positions. In the sequence below, I demonstrate how to execute the lift from the side bodylock position. Later in the book I will break down the importance of securing a dominant angle of attack prior to executing the lift, but when first starting out, it is important to focus on the lift itself. No matter what position you are executing the lift from, you must follow a few golden rules. The first rule is to position your hips directly underneath your opponent's hips. If you attempt to lift him with your legs and back, not only will you burn unnecessary energy, but you'll also increase your chance of injury. The second rule is to drive your hips forward as you lift your opponent off his feet. When you acquire the proper positioning and utilize proper technique, you should be able to lift a man more than twice your size with minimal effort.

I circle around to Ian's left side, position my hips underneath his hips, and secure a bodylock position by wrapping my arms around his waist. To close off all space between our bodies and make it difficult for him to escape my lock, I place my chest flush against his back.

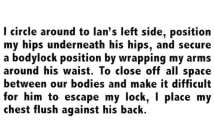

Keeping my arms wrapped tight around Ian's waist, I thrust my hips forward into his left side. It is important to note that the lift comes from my hips and not my legs. If you lift with your legs, you'll expend a considerable amount of energy.

Having driven my hips into Ian's side, I posture up and lift him into the air with little effort.

SEVENTH BASIC SKILL: HIP HEIST

The last basic skill is the hip heist, which is a technique that allows you to go from your back to your belly in one fluid movement. Like many of the basic skills in this section, the hip heist is used in many techniques, particularly when in guard or the bottom cross-body position. However, it is also frequently used when defending against takedowns. For example, if your opponent hauls you to the mat with a double-leg takedown, executing the hip heist before he can pin your back to the mat will often allow you to escape back to your feet or secure front head control. In the Takedown Defense section of this book, I demonstrate these two techniques, along with several others that incorporate the hip heist. To learn how the hip heist can be applied while grappling, visit my upcoming book devoted to ground techniques.

TECHNICAL NOTE: In the sequence below I offer two positions in which to finish the hip heist. If after executing the technique your chest is positioned over your opponent's back, you'll want to assume an offensive posture, which can be managed by remaining on all fours with your weight distributed evenly on each limb (see second-to-last photo). However, if after executing the hip heist your opponent's chest is on your back, you'll want to assume a defensive posture. This can be accomplished by dropping your butt down to your heels (see last photo).

I'm sitting on my butt with my hands and feet out in front of me.

I turn toward my left side and post my left hand on the mat behind me.

Still turning my body toward my left side, I push off the mat with my right foot, elevate my hips, and then keep my body suspended using my left arm.

Balancing on my left hand and right foot, I straighten my left leg out in front of me.

I rotate my body in a counterclockwise direction and chop my left leg into my right leg.

In one fluid motion, I twist my body in a counterclockwise direction, chop my left leg underneath my right leg, and turn my hips over so that I land on my hands and knees. It is important to note that I would assume this position if executing the hip heist put me on top of my opponent. For example, if I defended a takedown using the hip heist and then transitioned to head control, I would use this posture to secure the top position. To see how this technique is done, visit the section devoted to defending double-leg takedowns.

When I execute the hip heist and my opponent is still on top of me, I sit my butt to my heels and drop my chest to the mat to hinder him from securing control of my back.

1.2 BASIC POSITIONING

THE DOMINANT ANGLE

Early on in my wrestling career I realized the importance of creating dominant angles of attack. The majority of the time, you have a neutral angle. This is where your hips are square with your opponent, and his hips are square with you. It's considered a neutral angle because neither one of you has an advantage. If you shoot in for your opponent's legs, he can block you with his hands and sprawl his hips backward. If he shoots in for your legs, you can do the same. Instead of shooting blindly forward and confronting your opponent's power head on, a much better approach is to acquire a dominant angle, which is where your hips are facing your opponent, but his hips are facing away from you. When you shoot for your opponent's legs from a dominant angle, he doesn't have the ability to block you with his hands or sprawl his hips backward. Until he once again squares his hips up with your body, he's basically a sitting duck, making it very easy to penetrate in and then either drag him to the mat or hoist him into the air.

When I made the transition from wrestling to fighting, I brought this concept with me. I knew if I threw a punch or kick from a neutral angle, my opponent could block the strike using either his arms or legs. Instead of wasting energy throwing a bunch of strikes that had a small chance of landing, I sought to once again acquire a dominant angle. By moving off to my opponent's side, I could throw strikes that landed a large majority of the time. Until he adjusted his positioning and squared his hips with mine, he could do every little in the way of defense or counterstrikes.

The difficult part is not understanding why dominant angles are important, but rather becoming a master at creating them. If your opponent was locked into a fixed position, all you would have to do is move off to his side, but chances are he will track your movements to keep his hips square with your body. As a result, footwork alone often isn't enough. In order to create that dominant angle, you must use your hands to pull him off balance, throw feints, and set up your footwork using strikes. The better you become at distracting your opponent from your movements, the more luck you'll have at establishing that dominant angle. It is also important to note that once you do create a dominant angle, it usually won't last for long. Your opponent will realize that you've bypassed his defensive lines and quickly correct the positioning of his body. To avoid missing a golden opportunity, the instant you acquire a dominant angle, launch your attack. That attack could be in the form of punches, a kick, a dominant hold, or a takedown. For a brief second, you'll have free rein to do to your opponent as you will, so make use of it.

DOMINANT WRESTLING STANCE

NEUTRAL ANGLE

I'm squared off with Ian in my fighting stance.

DOMINANT ANGLE

To secure a dominant angle, I circle around to Ian's left side, grab his left biceps with my left hand, reach my right arm around his back, and cup my right hand around his right side. Notice how my hips are facing his body and his hips are turned away from me. Unable to block me with his hands or sprawl his hips away from me, I am free to drag him to the mat or hoist him into the air.

DOMINANT FIGHTING STANCE

NEUTRAL ANGLE

I'm squared off with Ian in my fighting stance.

DOMINANT ANGLE

To secure a dominant angle, I circle around to Ian's left side so that my hips are square with his body. With his hips facing away from me, the entire left side of his body is exposed. Until he readjusts and turns into me, he will have a very difficult time defending against my punches, kicks, or takedowns.

HEAD POSITIONING (THE POCKET)

When you obtain a dominant angle of attack and latch on to your opponent with an underhook or two-on-one control, head positioning is what will allow you to maintain control of his body. If your head is on the same horizontal plane as your opponent's head, he will be able to turn into you, square his hips with your hips, and return to a neutral angle. However, if you position your forehead in the gap between his head and near shoulder, an area I call "the pocket," your opponent will have a much more difficult time achieving his goal. It won't allow you to maintain the position forever, but it will give you a little extra time to execute your attack, as well as temporarily neutralize your opponent's attacks. So to reiterate, anytime you secure an underhook or two-on-one control, always work for a dominant angle with dominant head positioning.

I'm pointing to the pocket, which is located in the gap along Ian's neck between his right shoulder and ear.

To demonstrate proper head positioning, I place my forehead on the right side of Ian's neck between his shoulder and ear.

1.3 BASIC CONTROLS

INSIDE POSITIONING

Although most of the techniques in the following sections revolve around a specific control, such as two-on-one control, under-hook control, and head control, it is important that you understand the concept of inside positioning, which is when you position both of your hands to the inside of your opponent's arms. Technically, it's not a control position, but it puts you in a better position to attack your opponent or transition to one of the control positions just mentioned. I strongly suggest spending some time developing your ability to establish inside control because it gets you past your opponent's first line of defense, which is his arms, and gives you the inside line of attack. And anytime you get the inside line of attack, you are in a position to dominate your opponent.

I've secured inside control on Ian by positioning both of my arms to the inside of his arms and cupping my hands around the outside of his biceps.

TWO-ON-ONE CONTROL

Two-on-one control is when you latch on to one of your opponent's arms with both of your hands. You can establish these grips to serve as a form of control, as shown in the photos below, or you can establish these grips for the purpose of executing an arm drag, which will be covered later in the book. While I use two-on-one control more than any other control position in wrestling, I use it less than any other control when fighting. The reason for this is because in MMA your opponent is allowed to punch. If you have both of your hands gripping your opponent's right arm, he can punch you in the face with his left hand. Regardless of this fact, it is a very important control position to have in your arsenal. As long as you immediately execute your attack after establishing your grips, it can serve you well. Just as with all forms of control, head positioning is vital. By placing your head in the pocket between your opponent's head and near shoulder, you ensure dominant positioning. In the beginning, it is important to focus on the basic mechanics, which is what I demonstrate in the photos below. Later in the book, I show how to set up the control as well as what takedowns are available from the position.

To establish two-on-one control, I move toward Ian's right side, grip his right wrist with my right hand, cup my left hand around his upper right biceps, and pin his arm to my torso. To ensure dominant head positioning, I place my forehead in the pocket between his head and right shoulder. From here, I have several options to attack.

UNDERHOOK CONTROL

The underhook is another control that I use a lot in wrestling, but unlike two-on-one control, I use it all the time in fighting. When established properly, underhook control allows you to control one side of your opponent's body using just one arm, which leaves your other arm free to punch or attack with a takedown. The only catch is that you must secure a dominant underhook. If you look at the photos in the sequence below, you'll notice that there are two different types of underhooks—there is a dominant underhook and a weak underhook. To establish a dominant underhook, you must lift your opponent's arm up onto your shoulder and secure dominant head positioning. If you fail with these two tasks, your opponent can wrap his underhook arm over your arm and establish an overhook, which gives him several countering options. In addition to this, a weak underhook will give him enough space to pull his arm free and escape the position. As you will see later in the book, there are several ways to set up the underhook, as well as several attacks that you can employ from the underhook control position. To learn these setups and attacks, continue moving through the book sequentially.

WEAK UNDERHOOK CONTROL

I secure a left underhook by diving my left arm underneath Ian's right arm. To prevent me from establishing a dominant underhook, he positions his head underneath my head, giving him dominant head control. From this position, it will be very difficult for me to get my offense going.

DOMINANT UNDERHOOK CONTROL

I secure a left underhook by diving my left arm underneath Ian's right arm. To establish a dominant underhook, I position my head underneath his head, cup my left hand over his right shoulder, and lift his arm upward so that it is pinched between my head and shoulder. Assuming this position prevents him from wrapping his right arm around my left arm and securing an overhook. To hinder him from punching me with his free arm, I secure inside control by positioning my right arm to the inside of his left arm and placing my hand on his shoulder. From here, I have several options to attack.

HEAD CONTROL

I frequently utilize head control in both wrestling and MMA. Although there are many methods of controlling your opponent's head, I've found the method shown below to work best both on the wrestling mats and in the cage. Once you've established the position, you can secure chokes, strike with your knees, snap your opponent down to the mat, or transition to either two-on-one or underhook control. It is important to note that head control is not a technique that is necessarily set up. In most cases, you establish head control when countering your opponent's escape from two-on-one or underhook control. Later in the book I'll demonstrate ways to acquire the position, as well as the attacks that can be employed directly from the control. But just as with the other controls, it is important to focus on the actual hold when first starting out.

I cup my right hand underneath Ian's chin and cup my left hand around the back of his head. In these photos I am simply illustrating in detail how to position your hands to form the control. This is not a practical setup for the control position.

I use both of my arms to pull Ian's head into my belly. Notice how I've kept my elbows sucked in tight to my sides.

To secure dominant head control, I collapse my chest over the back of Ian's head. From here, I have several attack options, such as strikes, chokes, and takedowns. All of these options will be covered later in the book.

1.4 TWO-ON-ONE CONTROL SETUPS

CROSS GRIP

Utilizing the cross grip is a very basic but highly effective way to set up two-on-one control. To begin, reach your arm forward as if you are going to shake your opponent's lead hand and then grab his wrist. If your opponent has his right hand forward, grab his wrist using your right hand. If he has his left hand forward, grab his wrist with your left hand. Next, grab the outside of his lead elbow with your opposite hand. Once accomplished, secure a dominant angle of attack by moving to the outside of your opponent's body. And as always, secure the position by establishing dominant head control. Just as with the two-on-one shown earlier in the book, it is important to secure your opponent's arm to your chest and make it a part of your body. This will allow you to pull him off balance and set up a number of highly effective takedowns. What's nice about using the cross grip to two-on-one is that you don't need to readjust your grips as you assume a dominant angle. As you will see in the coming setups, this is rare.

I'm squared off with Ian in a wrestling stance, searching for an opening to attack. Both he and I are standing with right foot forward.

With Ian's right hand forward, I grab his right wrist with my right hand.

Maintaining a firm grip on Ian's right wrist, I cup my left hand around the back of his right elbow.

Having secured a two-on-one grip on Ian's right arm, I will now establish a dominant angle and secure two-on-one control. To begin, I step my left foot forward toward the outside of his right foot. At the same time, I pull his right arm toward my right side to disrupt his base.

Still pulling Ian's right arm toward my right side, I rotate my body in a clockwise direction and square my hips up with his to secure a dominant angle. To secure two-on-one control, I position my head in the pocket and pin his arm to my chest. From here, I will immediately initiate an attack.

ARM DRAG

The arm drag is essentially a form of two-on-one control because you have both hands on one of your opponent's arms, but it is important that you do not treat the arm drag position as a control position. The primary purpose of the arm drag is to set up a takedown or a control position such as two-on-one control or underhook control. In the sequence below, I show how to use it to establish two-on-one control, and later in the book I will demonstrate all of the takedown options that can be employed off the arm drag.

Ian has his left foot forward, putting him in a standard stance, and I have my right foot forward, putting me in a southpaw stance. Both of us are searching for an opening to attack.

I grab Ian's right wrist with my left hand.

To secure the arm drag position, I drive my right thumb into his right armpit and cup my fingers around the back of his arm.

In one fluid motion, I pull Ian's right arm toward my right side, step my left foot forward and to the outside of his right foot, turn my body in a clockwise direction, and place my head in the pocket on the right side of his head.

Having secured a dominant angle with dominant head positioning, all I have to do to secure two-on-one control is quickly switch my grip. To accomplish this, I slide my right hand down Ian's right arm and grab his wrist. At the same time, I move my left hand up his right arm and cup my hand around the inside of his upper arm. The instant I switch my grip, I pin his arm to my chest and secure two-on-one control. From here, I will immediately move forward with my attack.

INVERTED GRIP

Although I primarily use the inverted grip to set up two-on-one control while in the clinch, it can just as easily be done when there is space between you and your opponent. To make this transition, grab your opponent's near wrist so that your knuckles are facing the inside of your bodies, and then execute an arm drag to force movement. As your opponent counterbalances with a forward step, make your transition to two-on-one control. In the next sequence, I demonstrate how this same maneuver can be executed from the clinch.

I'm squared off with Ian, searching for an opening to attack.

To secure an inverted grip on Ian's lead arm, I grab his right wrist with my left hand. It is important to notice that my knuckles are pointing toward the inside of our bodies.

Keeping my left hand wrapped tightly around Ian's left wrist, I release my right grip and slide my right arm to the inside of his left arm, establishing an underhook.

To secure underhook control, I establish a dominant angle by circling my body in a counterclockwise direction, wrap my right arm around the back of Ian's left arm, cup my right hand over his left shoulder, and position my head in the pocket on the left side of his head. From here, I can immediately launch an attack.

INVERTED GRIP ARM DRAG

If you look at the second photo in the sequence below, you'll notice that I establish the arm drag position, but I form an inverted grip with my bottom hand. Although it's possible to execute an arm drag from this position and establish two-on-one control, as demonstrated in the previous section, I expect my opponent to resist the arm drag by pulling his arm in the opposite direction. The instant he takes the bait, I go with his pressure and force his arm toward the outside of his body. Having chosen an inverted grip, I can easily gain inside control by sliding my arm underneath his arm and establishing an underhook. If my opponent had not resisted the arm drag, my best course of action would have been to force his arm across his body and establish two-on-one control. To see how to accomplish this, revisit the previous section.

I'm squared off with Ian, searching for an opening to attack.

To begin my attack, I grab the inside of Ian's right wrist with my left hand (notice how my knuckles are facing the inside of our bodies.) Next, I secure the arm drag position by sliding my right hand up the inside of his right arm until my thumb is in his right armpit and then cup my fingers around the back of his upper triceps.

Realizing I am attempting to execute an arm drag, Ian counters my attack by pulling his right arm back. Instead of resisting his movements, I go with his momentum and dive my left hand to the inside of his right arm. Due to my inverted grip, this comes quite easily.

Circling my body in a clockwise direction to establish a dominant angle, I secure underhook control by wrapping my left arm around the back of Ian's right arm, cup my left hand over his shoulder, and position my head in the pocket on the right side of his head. From here, I can immediately get my offense going with an attack.

INSIDE POSITIONING TO UNDERHOOK CONTROL

As I have previously mentioned, securing inside control on your opponent's arms allows you to set up numerous attacks and controls. In this sequence, I demonstrate how to transition from inside control to underhook control. Although all the basic steps are included, it is important to note that you can get creative with this setup and others. For example, later in the book I show how to land an elbow to your opponent's face as you pummel from inside control to underhook control. Once you have spent some time learning the basics, I recommend experimenting as much as possible to learn what works best for you.

To secure inside control, I position both of my arms to the inside of Ian's arms.

In order to establish an underhook, I need to create space underneath one of Ian's arms. To accomplish this, I force his right arm upward by flaring my left elbow toward the ceiling. Notice how this exposes the right side of his body.

With Ian's right arm elevated, he is unable to defend against the underhook. To capitalize on this opening, I dive my left arm underneath his right arm.

Circling around to Ian's right side to secure a dominant angle of attack, I wrap my left arm around the back of his right arm and cup my left hand over his right shoulder. To prevent him from turning into me, I position my head in the pocket on his right side. To prevent him from wrapping his right arm over my left and establishing an overhook, I pinch his right arm between my left shoulder and head. From here, I have numerous attack options.

THE SWIM TECHNIQUE

The swim technique is one of the most common ways to secure underhook control from the over-under clinch position (the over-under position is a neutral position because you have one underhook and one overhook and your opponent has one underhook and one overhook). To execute the swim technique, take your hand and lay it flat to your chest. Then pummel your hand to the inside of your opponent's underhook arm. It's important to note that your opponent is going to try and do the same thing on the other side. To prevent him from achieving his goal, you want to rotate your body toward your underhook's side and step your rear leg forward to switch your stance. This will cut off all space between your bodies, making it very difficult for your opponent to swim his arm to the inside of your arm, which would neutralize your position and put you back to square one. Once you clear his arm you can secure dominant underhook control and immediately move forward into your attack. When studying the photos below, take notice of how I maintain inside control on my opponent's far arm with my free arm as I transition into the control.

I'm tied up with Ian in the clinch. We're in a neutral position because he has one underhook and I have one underhook. In order to transition to a dominant position, I have to clear his underhook. To begin this process, I lay my palm flat against my chest and slide it to the inside of his right shoulder.

I slide my left hand to the inside of Ian's right arm. It's important to notice how I keep my right arm hooked tight underneath his left arm and close off all space between our bodies. This prevents Ian from pummeling his left hand to the inside of my right arm and neutralizing the position.

Here I do several things at once. I step my left foot forward, and circle my body around to Ian's right side to create a dominant angle of attack. I wrap my left arm around Ian's left arm, cup my hand around his shoulder, and elevate my elbow—trapping his right arm between my left shoulder and neck. At the same time, I place my head in the pocket to his right side while maintaining inside control on his left arm with my right arm.

SHOULDER BUMP TO UNDERHOOK TRANSITION

Sometimes your opponent will pin his chest to your chest to remove all space between your bodies and prevent you from executing the swim technique. When faced with such a scenario, utilize the shoulder bump technique demonstrated below to create separation. Once accomplished, you can then employ the swim technique to secure underhook control.

I'm tied up with Ian in the cinch. We both have an underhook, putting us in a neutral position. Notice how we are chest to chest.

To be able to utilize the swim technique, I need to create separation between our bodies. I accomplish this by throwing my right shoulder forward into Ian's body. It is important to mention that this is an explosive movement, just like snapping your fist at the end of a punch.

Having created space between our bodies, I flatten my left palm flush against my chest and then begin digging it into the crevice in front of Ian's right arm.

I dive my left arm to the inside of Ian's right arm.

I wrap my left arm over Ian's right arm, cup my hand over his right shoulder, elevate my left elbow, and then shrug my left shoulder. Notice how these actions pin his right arm between my left shoulder and neck, preventing him from overhooking my left arm and tightening down on my underhook with a whizzer.

I step my left foot forward and circle around to Ian's right side, creating a dominant angle of attack. To secure underhook control, I position my head in the pocket on his right side while maintaining inside control on his left arm with my right arm. From here, I have several options to attack.

1.6: TRANSITIONING TO CONTROL POSITIONS

TWO-ON-ONE CONTROL TO UNDERHOOK

As I mentioned in the introduction to this section, all the control positions offered in this book are connected, which means you can transition back and forth between them. Deciding what transition to make should be based upon your opponent's defense. For example, in the sequence below, I secure two-on-one control, and my opponent defends by backing away. This action causes his head to drop, which offers me an easy transition to head control. To defend against my head control, he pulls his head up and away, which allows me to make another transition to underhook control. Anytime your opponent attempts to strip you of one control, he's vulnerable to another form of control, but in order to capitalize on this weakness, you must have your transitions down pat.

I've secured two-on-one control on Ian's right side.

In an attempt to escape my control, Ian creates separation between our bodies by stepping his right foot back. This action causes him to bend forward at the waist, giving me an opportunity to make a smooth transition to head control.

I begin transitioning to head control by grabbing the back of Ian's head with my left hand and applying downward pressure.

To secure head control, I collapse my chest over the back of Ian's head, wrap my right arm around his neck, and cup his chin with my right hand.

Before I can implement an attack from head control, Ian pulls his head free by rotating his body in a clockwise direction.

To capitalize on Ian's positioning, I wrap my right arm over his left arm and cup my right hand over his left shoulder, securing an underhook. Notice how this traps his left arm between my neck and shoulder, preventing him from cinching down on my underhook arm with a tight whizzer.

With my right elbow still elevated to keep Ian's left arm trapped between my shoulder and neck, I step my right foot to the outside of his body and circle around his left foot, giving me a dominant angle. At the same time, I move my left arm to the inside of his right arm, supplying me with inside positioning.

UNDERHOOK TO HEAD CONTROL TO TWO-ON-ONE CONTROL

By now you understand how important it is to use your opponent's defense against your initial control position to transition into a secondary control position. If he defends against your secondary control position, you transition into a third. These reactionary transitions are what allow you to remain on the offensive. Remember, you always want to take what your opponent gives you. Never force a position. In the sequence below, I transition from underhook control to head control to two-on-one control and then back to head control, all based upon my opponent's defense to each position.

I've secured underhook control on Ian's left side.

Ian escapes my control by stepping his left foot back. This causes his head to drop toward the mat, creating an opportunity for me to transition into head control.

To capitalize on Ian's positioning, I grab the back of his head with left hand and apply downward pressure. Notice that I've kept my right hand cupped around the back of his left shoulder.

To secure head control, I collapse my chest over the back of Ian's head, wrap my right arm around his neck, and cup his chin with my right hand.

Before I can launch an attack from head control, Ian pulls his head free by rotating his body in a counterclockwise direction.

As Ian backs away, I grab his right wrist using my right hand and hook my left hand around the back of his upper right arm. Notice that I've positioned my left thumb in his armpit.

I secure two-on-one control by stepping my left foot forward and to the outside of Ian's right leg, positioning my head in the pocket, and pinning his arm to my chest. My ultimate goal is to immediately begin working for a takedown, but if Ian should defend against my position, I will transition to another control.

HEAD CONTROL TO UNDERHOOK CONTROL TO TWO-ON-ONE

This is another example of how to transition from one control position to another based upon your opponent's defenses. From the clinch, my opponent pulls his hips back and drops his head, allowing me to secure head control. But I am not in love with that head. When he pulls his head up and away to escape my control, I have an opening to transition to either two-on-one control or underhook control. In the sequence below, I choose underhook control. From there, my opponent defends against my position, and I make yet another transition to two-on-one control. I realize that putting in so many transitions might seem like overkill, but it is extremely important to understand how to transition back and forth between the different control positions. Once you grasp this concept and can put it into action, executing takedowns or strikes from the clinch will be a lot easier to manage.

I've secured head control on Ian.

Before I can implement an attack from head control, Ian pulls his head free by rotating his body in a clockwise direction. As he backs away, I shoot my right arm underneath his left arm.

I step forward and maneuver my body around to Ian's left side. As I move into a dominant angle, I secure a right underhook by wrapping my right arm over the top of his left arm and cupping his shoulder with my right hand.

Sensing danger, Ian quickly steps his left foot back in an attempt to escape underhook control. As he creates separation between our bodies, I latch on to the back of his right elbow with my left hand.

I establish a two-on-one grip on Ian's right arm by grabbing on to his right wrist with my right hand.

I secure two-on-one control by stepping my left foot forward and to the outside of Ian's right leg, positioning my head in the pocket, and pinning his arm to my chest. From here, I will immediately work for an attack based off his reaction to the position.

PART TWO: TAKEDOWN SETUPS

OVERVIEW

If you studied chapter 1, you now understand how to set up and secure two-on-one control, underhook control, and head control. In this chapter, I demonstrate the attacks that are available from each of these positions. You will learn how to set up the single-leg takedown position, the double-leg takedown position, and back control. You will also learn how to execute techniques such as the knee pick and slide-by. As you will soon discover, the same techniques are employed from each of the three control positions—the only difference is the starting position and how you set them up. For example, I demonstrate how to utilize the slide-by from two-on-one control, underhook control, and head control. This is vastly superior than trying to learn a whole new group of techniques from each control position because all you have to do is alter the setups. Once you understand the dynamics behind a certain technique, you can apply it to almost every clinching scenario. It is important to note that throughout this section, anytime a move takes you to a double-leg, single-leg, or back control, the move ends at the beginning of that control. The reason for this is that each position offers multiple finishing options. To make learning those options as simple as possible, I have organized them into their own sections later in the book.

ARM DRAG TECHNIQUES (p. 55-64)

When you establish two-on-one control, an excellent option is to pull on your opponent's arm using an arm drag. The majority of the time this will cause him to instinctively pull his arm back toward his body, allowing you to execute a number of takedowns, including the high dive, double-leg, and single-leg. His reaction also creates an opening for the slide-by, which can be used to take him to the mat or transition to back control. While the arm drag is a rather simple technique, there are a few key points that must be followed. Regardless of whether your initial grip is a near grip or inverted grip, you must drive the thumb of your opposite hand up into your opponent's armpit and form a grip around his upper triceps. If you establish your second grip low on his arm, which is a common mistake, you won't have the control you need to execute a proper arm drag. Instead of moving his entire body, you'll only move his arm, which won't invoke the needed reaction from your opponent. The second key to success is to release your opponent's arm the instant he resists the arm drag. If your timing is off, your opponent will readjust his base, eliminating the opening to attack with the aforementioned techniques.

UNDERHOOK TECHNIQUES (p. 66-74)

This section is devoted to the attacks that can be implemented from underhook control. In the first sequence presented, I demonstrate how to use the position to secure a bodylock and haul your opponent to the mat. This should be your primary objective. However, if your opponent should mount an escape before

you can execute this initial attack, I demonstrate numerous ways to use his escape to your advantage. Depending upon how he attempts to strip your control, you can execute a double-leg takedown, a single-leg takedown, or transition to his back. These techniques are the same options that you had off the arm drag from two-on-one control, but here you learn how to set them up off your opponent's escape from underhook control. Although it is important to master each of these options to prepare yourself for any scenario, you do not want to wait for your opponent to make his escape. Assuming underhook control makes him extremely vulnerable, and you always want to use that vulnerability to immediately attack. The only reason to employ one of the alternate attacks is when your opponent manages to beat you to the punch with his escape. As he turns into you to eliminate your dominant angle, change your level, penetrate into his body, and take him to the mat. Your success with these techniques will be measured by your ability to time his escape and execute your attack before he can reestablish his base.

HEAD CONTROL TECHNIQUES (p. 77-86)

This section covers the attacks that are available from head control. The instant you secure this position, your primary objective is to execute the snap down, which is the first technique presented. If your opponent should mount an escape before you can utilize the snap down, use his escape to transition into one of the subsequent attacks. Just as with two-on-one and underhook control, deciding which attack to utilize should be based upon your opponent's chosen method of escape. Again, the options at your disposal are the same as with the previous two control positions, but here you learn how to set them up from head control.

2.1: TWO-ON-ONE TECHNIQUES (ARM DRAG)

ARM DRAG TO HIGH DIVE

As you now know, when you attack your opponent with an arm drag, he will usually defend by pulling his arm back. This gives you several options to attack, but my personal favorite is to execute a high dive. Not only is it a high-percentage takedown that is easy to finish, but it is also conducive to my posture off the arm drag. Anytime I pull my opponent's arm toward the outside of my body while in an elevated stance, I will always attack his hips with the high dive because it doesn't require me to change my level before penetrating into his comfort zone—I can transition right into the technique from a high stance. If you prefer to attack your opponent's lower body with single- or double-leg takedowns, then you'll want to pull his arm down and drop your level into a low stance when executing the arm drag. This will allow you to penetrate into his comfort zone as he defends, which I demonstrate over the coming pages. The key to success with the high dive, as well as the other takedowns covered in this section, is to release the arm drag the instant your opponent begins pulling his arm back. When timed correctly, his head will pop up and his hips will shoot forward, allowing you to penetrate through his lines of defense and secure the takedown.

I'm squared off with Ian, searching for an opening to attack.

I secure the two-on-one arm drag position by latching on to Ian's right wrist with my left hand and cupping my right hand around the inside of his right arm. The instant I secure this grip, I pull his arm toward my right side.

To prevent me from pulling him off balance, Ian yanks his right arm back. Instead of resisting his pull, I release my grips on his right arm.

As Ian pulls his right arm back in defense, I drop my level and penetrate into his body by stepping my right leg deep between his legs and positioning my head in the center of his chest.

I wrap both of my arms around Ian's waist and then cross my arms. Notice how I grab my right forearm with my left hand and grab my left forearm with my right hand.

Having secured a tight bodylock, I drive off the mat using my right foot and begin lifting Ian upward.

I continue to lift Ian upward.

I achieve full lift by stepping my right leg back. From here, I can slam Ian to the mat and achieve top control.

ARM DRAG TO DOUBLE-LEG

As I mentioned in the previous introduction, when you secure the arm drag your opponent's natural reaction will be to yank his arm back to prevent you from pulling him off balance. In the last sequence, I used the arm drag to pull my opponent's arm toward the outside of my body, and then used his defense to shoot forward and set up the high dive. Here I secure the same arm drag position, but instead of pulling his arm toward the outside of my body, I pull it straight down toward the mat. As he pulls his arm up in defense, I keep my elevation low and shoot forward to set up the double-leg takedown. Neither technique is better than the other. Deciding which one to use boils down to what you feel more comfortable with. In this technique you pull your opponent's arm down, position your head to the outside of his body, and attack low. In the previous technique you pull his arm to the side, position your head in the center of his chest, and attack higher up on his hips.

I'm squared off with Ian, searching for an opening to attack.

I secure the two-on-one arm drag position by latching on to Ian's right wrist with my left hand and cupping my right hand around the inside of his right arm. The moment I secure this grip, I drop my elevation and pull his arm down toward the mat.

Keen to my actions, Ian pulls his right arm back in defense. Instead of resisting his movement, I release my grip on his right arm. Because I timed his reaction properly, Ian's head pops up and his hips come forward. It's important to notice how I've stayed low. This puts me in a perfect position to shoot in for a double-leg takedown.

As Ian pulls his arm back, I shoot forward, step my right leg deep between his legs, wrap my arms around the back of his knees, and position my head to the outside of his right hip. It's important to notice that my back is straight and my head is up. From here, I can take Ian to the mat using a double-leg finish. To see these finishes, flip to the section devoted to double-leg takedowns.

ARM DRAG TO HIGH SINGLE

The single-leg takedown is set up in the same manner as the double-leg takedown in that you secure the two-on-one arm drag position, yank your opponent's arm down toward the mat, and then use his defensive reaction to your advantage by shooting into his comfort zone. However, instead of positioning your head to the outside of his body and attacking with a double-leg, you position your head to the inside of his body and attack with a single-leg. When deciding which takedown to implement, always refer to your opponent's stance. If he is standing in an opposite stance to you, meaning he has his opposite leg forward, then you always want to attack his lead leg and set up the single-leg takedown. If he is standing in the same stance as you, meaning he has the same foot forward, then you always want to attack with a double-leg takedown.

Ian is standing in a standard stance with his left leg forward, and I'm standing in a southpaw stance with my right leg forward. Both of us are looking for an opening to attack.

To begin my attack, I latch on to Ian's left wrist with my right hand so that my knuckles are facing the inside of our bodies. Next, I bring my left hand to the inside of his left arm until my thumb hits his armpit. To secure the arm drag position, I cup my left hand around the back of his upper triceps.

The moment I secure the arm drag position, I drop my level and pull Ian's arm down toward the mat. Keen to my actions, Ian pulls his right arm back in defense. Instead of resisting his movement, I release my grip on his left arm. Having timed his reaction properly, his head pops up and his hips come forward. It's important to notice how I've stayed low. This puts me in a perfect position to shoot in for a single-leg takedown.

To set up the single-leg takedown, I penetrate into Ian's comfort zone by stepping my right foot to the outside of his left leg and positioning my head in the center of his chest. At the same time, I wrap my right arm around the back of his left hip and my left arm around the inside of his left leg. Next, I secure my control on his leg by gripping the top of my left wrist with my right hand. It's important to notice that my back is straight and my head is up. From this position I have several options to attack. To see these finishes, flip to the section devoted to single-leg takedowns.

REACH AROUND TO BACK CONTROL

I call this technique the reach around. Despite it's name, it has nothing to do with homosexuality. It's set up off the arm drag like the previous moves, but in this situation your opponent fails to defend against the arm drag by yanking his arm back, allowing you to move into the two-on-one control position. If you have your opponent's right arm controlled as I do in the photos below, the next step is to reach your left arm around his back and to his far hip. Once accomplished, keep your head in position, slightly drop your elevation, and circle around toward his back. To see your finishing options, flip to the section devoted to back control finishes.

I'm squared off with Ian. To set up the arm drag, I grab his right wrist with my left hand.

Keeping a firm grip on Ian's right wrist with my left hand, I secure the arm drag by bringing my right hand to the inside of his right arm until my thumb hits his armpit.

As I wrap my right hand around Ian's upper right triceps, I rotate my body in a clockwise direction, step my left foot forward, and pull his right arm down and toward my right side. Notice that I position my head in the pocket on his right side.

I release my left grip on Ian's right wrist.

Still pulling Ian's right arm toward the right side of my body using my right hand, I reach my left arm around his back and hook my hand on his left side.

Having pulled Ian off balance using the arm drag, I step my left foot forward, wrap my right arm around the front of his waist, grip my right wrist with my left hand, and secure control of his back. From here, I have several options to attack.

SLIDE-BY TO BACK CONTROL

In this scenario, you're tied up with your opponent in the clinch with one overhook and one underhook. From this position, an excellent option is to utilize a slide-by, a highly effective wrestling maneuver that translates well to MMA. To set it up, secure the basic arm drag position, but instead of executing the drag, drop your level and slide your head down your opponent's underhook arm. Once you've trapped his arm to the side of his body using your head, it becomes very easy to circle around to his back and secure back control. From there, you can immediately work on hauling him to the mat.

I'm tied up with Ian in the clinch. We're in a neutral position because we both have an overhook and an underhook.

I secure the arm drag position by latching on to Ian's right wrist with my left hand and cupping my right hand around the inside of his right arm.

Instead of dragging Ian's arm across my body, I release my grip, drop my level, slide my head down his right arm, wrap my right arm around the left side of his waist, and penetrate into his comfort zone by stepping my right foot deep between his legs. With these actions, I trap his right arm to the right side of his body.

Rotating my body in a clockwise direction, I pull down on Ian's left hip using my left hand, step my left foot forward, and circle around toward his back. At the same time, I drive my head toward the center of his back and close off all space between our bodies.

I continue to circle around Ian's right side toward his back. To secure back control, I wrap my left arm around his left side and latch on to my left wrist with my right hand. Notice that I've collapsed my chest over his back, keeping all space closed off between our bodies. From here, I have several finishing options. To see these finishes, flip to the section devoted to back control finishes.

2.2: UNDERHOOK TECHNIQUES

UNDERHOOK TO HIGH SINGLE

In this sequence I demonstrate how to secure the single-leg takedown off dominant underhook control. All it involves is reaching down and obtaining control of your opponent's near leg, making it one of the easiest takedowns to set up from the dominant underhook position. The key to being successful with this technique is closing off all space between your bodies by stepping your lead leg behind your opponent's far leg. If you accomplish this, your opponent's near leg becomes very easy to snare. However, if your opponent defends against your dominant underhook control by stepping his lead leg back before you have a chance to secure the position, you will have to execute one of the subsequent techniques.

I've secured underhook control on Ian's left side.

Keeping Ian's left arm pinned between my shoulder and neck and maintaining inside control on his right arm using my left arm, I drop my level and step my right leg behind his right foot. With this action, I have effectively closed off all space between our bodies.

I wrap my right arm around the back of Ian's left leg.

To secure single-leg control, I wrap my right arm around the back of Ian's left hip, hook my left arm around the inside of his left knee, and then grip my hands together. Notice how my back is straight, my head is up, and my right ear is pinned to his chest. To see how to finish the single-leg, flip to the section devoted to single-leg takedowns.

BODYLOCK TAKEDOWN FROM UNDERHOOK CONTROL

The bodylock takedown is another excellent technique to utilize from underhook control. It is very similar to the single-leg in that you must secure the takedown before your opponent can defend against your dominant position by stepping back, squaring his hips with your hips, and clearing your control. Where it differs from the single-leg is that instead of locking your arms around your opponent's near leg, you lock your arms around his waist and secure a bodylock. To get the takedown from this position, pull his hips into your body, pressure your head into his chest, and haul him to the mat.

I've secured underhook control on Ian's left side.

I drop my level, wrap my right arm around Ian's back, wrap my left arm around his abdomen, and secure a bodylock by gripping my hands together over his right hip.

The moment I secure the bodylock, I pull Ian's hips into my body, drive my head into his chest, and pinch my knees together around his left leg. The first two actions cause him to arch backward and lose balance, while the last action prevents him from stepping back and regaining his balance.

4

Having established a bodylock and broken Ian's base, I step my left leg behind his left leg and start hauling him to the mat.

5

As I step my right foot forward, Ian falls toward the mat.

6

I follow Ian to the mat and establish the cross-body position.

UNDERHOOK TO DOUBLE-LEG

When you establish underhook control you are in a very dominant position, but you must attack quickly. With your opponent having very few options at his disposal, the majority of the time he will attempt to break your control and eliminate your dominant angle by turning his hips toward your hips and backing away. If you are unable to attack your opponent before he can make his escape, it is very important to attack him as he is making his escape. While he is in transition, there is an assortment of attacks that you can utilize, such as the double-leg takedown demonstrated in the sequence below, but they are only available for a very brief window. In order to capitalize on them, you must drill this technique and others like it until you can read your opponent's movements and anticipate his reactions. If you fail to execute your attack the moment he begins exiting your control, you're going to lose your opening, putting you back to square one.

I've secured an underhook on Ian's left side.

In an attempt to free his left arm and clear my control, Ian steps his left foot back and switches his stance.

As Ian clears my underhook control, I drop my level and flare my left elbow up toward the ceiling. Having maintained inside control on his right arm, this action causes his right arm to elevate, creating an opening for the double-leg takedown.

Keeping my left arm elevated and continuing to drop my level by sinking my hips toward the mat, I penetrate into Ian's comfort zone by stepping my right leg to the inside of his right leg, ducking my head underneath his right arm, and wrapping my right arm around his left side.

I continue to shoot forward by driving off the mat with my left foot. To set up the double-leg, I slip my head underneath Ian's right arm and hook both of my arms around the back of his legs. It's important to note that I'm driving my right shoulder into Ian's right side, keeping my back straight and my head up. By maintaining strong posture, I prevent Ian from wrapping his right arm around my neck and choking me with a guillotine.

SLIDE-BY TO BACK CONTROL

It's important to remember that your opponent is never going to let you stay at a dominant angle for long. It doesn't matter if he is a fighter or not—it's not in human nature. For example, if you're shaking someone's hand and you suddenly take an angle on him, it will make him feel uncomfortable. Most likely, he will square his body back up with yours. So again, you always have to anticipate your opponent trying to come back to that neutral angle. In this sequence, you've secured underhook control and once again your opponent tries to clear your control by stepping back and turning his hips to face your hips. As he does this, you immediately shoot in and take his back. As you may have noticed, I'm showing the same takedown setups from the underhook as I did from the two-on-one arm drag position. I do the same techniques off all of the basic controls positions, which is what makes them work. I don't make up a bunch of complicated techniques that change from control position to control position. Instead I have fundamentally sound techniques that work effectively from all the controls.

I've secured underhook control on Ian's left side.

In an attempt to free his left arm and strip me of my dominant angle, Ian steps his left foot back and turns his hips toward my hips. Notice how by stepping back he switches his stance.

As Ian turns to face me, I drop my level and penetrate into his comfort zone by driving my left foot off the mat and stepping my right leg deep between his legs. At the same time, I wrap my right arm around the left side of his waist and pin his right arm to the side of his body using my head. It's important to notice that I maintain solid posture by keeping my back straight and my head up.

Rotating my body in a counterclockwise direction, I pull down on Ian's left hip with my right hand and circle around toward his back. At the same time, I drive my head toward the center of his back, keeping his arm trapped to his side and closing off all space between our bodies.

I continue to circle around Ian's right side toward his back. To secure back control, I step my left leg forward, wrap my left arm around his left side, and grab my left wrist with my right hand. Notice that I've collapsed my chest over his back, closing off all space between our bodies. From here, I have several finishing options. To see these finishes, flip to the section devoted to back control finishes.

KNEE PICK FROM UNDERHOOK CONTROL

The knee pick from underhook control is another technique that I use a lot in MMA. In contrast to the double-leg and slide-by, the key here is to not run through your opponent's body. Instead, you want to run past him, hauling him to the mat as you go. Following this rule will prevent your feet from getting tangled up with his, which will cause you to lose your balance and fail with the takedown. As long as you run past his body instead of plowing into it, you will most likely take your opponent to the mat and land in a dominant position.

I've secured underhook control on Ian's left side.

In an attempt to free his left arm and strip me of my dominant angle, Ian steps his left foot back and turns his hips toward my hips.

The moment Ian steps back to face me, I drop my level, wrap my right arm around his left hip, and hook my left hand around the outside of his right knee. It's important to notice the angle of my body in relation to Ian's. From here, I will run forward as if I were following an imaginary horizontal line that is separating our bodies.

I step my right foot in front of my left foot, drive my right arm into Ian's left side, and chop my left hand into his right knee.

Continuing to drive my right arm into Ian's left side and chop my left hand into his right knee, I step my left foot in front of my right foot. Because I was fluid with my movements and ran my body past Ian's body, he plummets to the mat and falls on his right side.

As Ian lands on the mat, I drop toward my right knee and start working to secure the cross-body position.

To secure the cross-body position and pin Ian to the mat, I drop to my knees, wrap my left arm around the right side of his head, wrap my right arm underneath his left arm, and grip my hands together under his left shoulder.

2.3: HEAD CONTROL TECHNIQUES

SNAP DOWN TO SPIN AROUND

From head control, I will usually attack with the snap down. To execute this technique effectively, you want to move your body back while pulling your opponent's head down toward the mat. When you do this, one of two things will happen. Either he will protect his face from hitting the mat by placing his hands on the ground or he will pull his head back to resist. If he chooses the former option, use the technique demonstrated in the sequence below to spin around his side and take control of his back. If he chooses the latter option, you will want to transition to a single- or double-leg takedown, which I demonstrate how to do in the following sequences.

I've secured head control on Ian.

To create distance, I step my left foot straight back.

3

As I step back, I sink my hips and pull Ian's head down toward the mat. To protect his face from hitting the mat, he places both of his hands on the ground. It's important to note that I'm using the momentum of my backward step to maximize my pulling power and haul my opponent to the mat.

4

Still pulling Ian's head to the mat using my control, I take another step back and pull him down on to all fours.

5

I collapse my chest over Ian's back.

6

Keeping my weight centered over Ian's back, I circle around to his left side, wrap my right arm around his right side, post my right knee next to his left leg, and establish control of his back.

SNAP DOWN TO DOUBLE-LEG

When you utilize the snap down and your opponent resists by pulling his head backward, it creates an opportunity to execute a double- or single-leg takedown. In this sequence, I demonstrate how to employ a double-leg takedown, which is most effective when your opponent is in the same stance as you. If your opponent is standing in an opposite stance, meaning with his opposite foot forward, then you will want to shoot in the single-leg takedown demonstrated in the following sequence. The key to being successful with either technique is to let go of your opponent's head the instant he resists the snap down. When your release is timed properly, his head will snap back, creating an opening for the takedown. However, his head will not remain in this position for long, making it important to immediately penetrate in. The more you hesitate, the less likely you will be to finish the takedown.

I've secured head control on Ian.

To execute the snap down, I step my left foot back and pull Ian's head toward the mat.

To keep from getting hauled to the mat, Ian pulls his head back. Instead of resisting, I release my control of his head, causing his head to pop upward. It's important to notice that I've kept my level low so that I can immediately penetrate into his comfort zone.

Driving off my left foot, I step my right leg between Ian's legs. As I penetrate into his comfort zone, I wrap my right arm around his left hip and my left arm around his right leg. It's important to notice that my head is up and my back is straight. From here, I can take him to the mat utilizing a double-leg takedown. To see your finishing options from this position, flip to the section devoted to double-leg finishes.

SNAP DOWN TO HIGH SINGLE

This technique is utilized in the same scenario as the last. From the front headlock position, you pull your opponent's head downward utilizing the snap down, and he resists by pulling his head backward, creating an opportunity for a takedown. However, in this scenario your opponent has his opposite foot forward. Instead of utilizing a double-leg, which is best employed when your opponent has the same foot forward, you utilize a single-leg takedown. Just as with the double-leg, you want to let go of your opponent's head as he resists the snap down, remain low, and quickly shoot in for the takedown.

I've secured control of Ian's head. Notice that we're standing with the opposite feet forward. Due to this fact, I will shoot in with the single-leg and attack his lead leg.

To execute the snap down, I step my left foot back and pull Ian's head toward the mat.

To keep from getting hauled to the mat, Ian pulls his head back. Instead of resisting his pressure, I release control of his head, causing it to pop upward. It's important to notice that I've kept my level low so I can immediately penetrate into his comfort zone.

I slide my left foot up to my right heel.

I step my right foot forward and to the outside of Ian's left leg. To secure the high single position, I wrap my right arm around the back of Ian's left hip, hook my left arm around the inside of his left knee, and then grip my hands together. Notice how my back is straight, my head is up, and my right ear is pinned to his chest. To see how to finish the single-leg, flip to the section devoted to single-leg takedowns.

DOUBLE-LEG

When you establish a dominant control, your opponent has to escape that control before he can attack. Anticipating his escape and using his exit strategy as a means of setting up your attack has been an ongoing theme throughout this book. You used it from two-on-one control and underhook control, and now you are going to use it again from head control. When you secure head control, your opponent's most common defense will be to grab your hand so that he can free his head, pull his chin up, and back away. However, while your opponent is making his escape, he is very vulnerable to the double-leg takedown demonstrated below. The key to success is to keep your elevation low and immediately transition into the takedown.

I've secured head control on Ian.

In an attempt to escape, Ian latches on to my right wrist with both of his hands.

Ian rips my right hand off of his chin. Notice that I've kept my left arm hooked around the back of his head.

To clear my control, Ian pulls his head out from underneath my body. Immediately I redirect his head toward my right using my left arm.

I penetrate into Ian's comfort zone by driving off my left foot and stepping my right leg between his legs. It's important to note that I am driving my right shoulder into his right side, trapping his arm to the side of his body.

As I penetrate into Ian's comfort zone, I wrap my right arm around his left hip and my left arm around his right leg. From here I can finish him with a double-leg takedown. To see your finishing options from this position, flip to the section devoted to double-leg finishes.

HEAD CONTROL TO HIGH SINGLE

This technique begins the same as the previous one. You secure head control on your opponent, and he attempts to escape by ripping your bottom hand off his chin and pulling his head upward. The only difference is that here your opponent is standing in an opposite stance. As you learned in previous techniques, when your opponent has the same foot forward you shoot for the double, and when he has his opposite foot forward you shoot for the single. It's no different here.

I've secured head control on Ian. Notice that we are standing in opposite stances.

In order to escape my control, Ian has to free his head. To begin this process, he latches on to my right arm with both of his hands.

3.1: DOUBLE-LEG FINISHES

DRIVE-THROUGH DOUBLE-LEG FINISH

When you penetrate into your opponent for a double-leg takedown and manage to get his momentum moving backward, your easiest route for finishing the takedown is to use your forward momentum to force him to the mat. As you will see in the sequence below, this allows you to immediately secure side control, pin your opponent, and begin landing strikes or working for a submission. However, if your goal is to take your opponent down but remain standing, you'll want to use the next technique in this section.

I've managed to secure the double-leg position on Ian.

I step my left foot forward and to the outside of Ian's right foot.

Continuing to drive forward, I step my right foot in front of my left foot and in between Ian's legs. It's important to note that I am chopping both of my arms into the back of his legs to prevent him from sprawling his legs back and blocking the takedown.

Due to my forward drive, Ian falls flat to his back.

As Ian's back hits the mat, I follow him down by positioning my head to the right side of his body, wrapping my right arm around his left hip, and sliding my right shin over his left leg. As a rule of thumb, you always want to position your head to the opposite side from which you are passing. In this case, I'm passing toward my opponent's left side so I position my head on his right.

6

Keeping the weight of my body distributed over Ian's torso, I slide my right leg over his left leg and begin circling my body in a counterclockwise direction. At the same time, I throw my left leg over his left leg and pin my left elbow to his left hip.

7

To secure the cross-body position, I open my base and drop all of my weight over Ian's abdomen and hips. From here, I can begin my attack from the cross-body position.

DRIVE-THROUGH DOUBLE-LEG FINISH (DUMP THE RIDER)

In the previous sequence I demonstrated how to complete the double-leg takedown by continuing to drive into your opponent, haul him to the mat, and secure the top position. The only difference with this technique is that you remain on your feet as you drive your opponent to the mat. While the former might be a better option for a wrestling match, the one demonstrated in this sequence might be considered a better option for a fight because you are in a good position to land hard strikes. It all depends upon your goals and the opponent you are fighting. As with most techniques that have multiple ways to finish, the path you choose boils down to personal preference.

I've managed to penetrate into Ian's comfort zone with the double-leg.

To finish the takedown, I step my left foot to the outside of Ian's right leg, drive my right shoulder into the center of his chest, and chop both of my arms into the back of his legs.

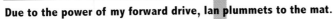

Due to the power of my forward drive, Ian plummets to the mat.

As Ian hits the mat, I posture up and cup the back of his heels with my hands. From here, I will clear his legs and either start to throw hard punches or pass his guard to secure a more dominant position.

DOUBLE-LEG LIFT AND SWING FINISH

In the "Seven Basic Skills" section of this book, I covered the "lift" and the importance of pulling your head up and thrusting your hips forward. Here we put this skill to use in the double-leg lift and swing finish. The main thing to remember is to keep your opponent's hips drawn in tight to your body. If he manages to sprawl his legs back and sink his hips, the takedown will be lost. To execute this technique correctly, you want to step your rear leg up so that you are square with your opponent's hips. Once you establish a firm base, lift him into the air and then swing his leg past your body. Next, forcefully throw him to the mat while remaining standing. The moment he hits the mat, drop down and cover his body to secure top control. As with all the techniques in this book, executing each step in one fluid motion is mandatory.

I've secured the double-leg position on Ian.

I step my left foot forward and to the outside of Ian's right leg.

Keeping my head up and driving my hips forward, I use both of my arms to heft Ian up off the mat.

Still driving my hips forward and keeping my eyes pointing toward the ceiling, I straighten my legs and hoist Ian up on to my right shoulder.

As I lift Ian into the air, I swing his body toward my left side by rotating my shoulders in a counterclockwise direction and pulling on his left leg with my left hand.

I drop Ian to the mat.

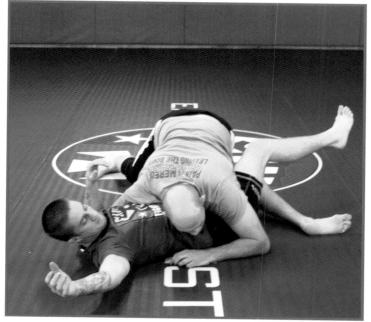

The moment Ian hits the mat, I assume the cross-body position by dropping my chest to his chest, distributing all of my weight over his torso, and pinning my left knee to his left hip.

TURNING THE CORNER

The "turning the corner" finish is all about taking an angle on your opponent. The moment you penetrate in for the double-leg, you immediately want to turn your body as if you were trying to read what's on the back of your opponent's shirt. When you can properly see his back, you know the takedown is fully executable. That's when you want to drive through him and take him to the mat. However, it is important to avoid your opponent's legs. Just like the knee pick, you want to run past his feet to avoid tripping yourself up and losing balance.

I've secured the double-leg on Ian.

I turn my body in a counterclockwise direction and drive my head into Ian's right side. Notice how this action turns him toward his left and throws him off balance.

As I continue to turn my body in a counterclockwise direction, I wrap my left arm around the back of Ian's right leg and place my right hand on the outside of his left knee. It is important to note that I do not stop turning until I can read what's on the back of his shirt.

Having turned the corner on Ian, I step my left foot in front of my right, chop my right hand into his left knee, and drive him to the mat. Notice how I avoid his feet by running past him instead of driving through him.

I follow Ian to the mat and secure the cross-body position.

DUMP THE RIDER (DEFENDING THE GUILLOTINE)

Throughout this book, I've stressed the importance of keeping your head up and your back straight when shooting in for the double-leg. Maintaining proper form not only makes the takedown easier to manage, but it also prevents your opponent from wrapping his arm around your neck and cinching in a guillotine choke. However, even with perfect form, your opponent will sometimes still manage to secure the submission. In such a scenario, you immediately want to protect your neck by establishing a two-on-one grip on his arm. This removes you from the danger zone and allows you to take an angle and dump your opponent to the mat. If you forget this defense and continue with your original takedown or lift your opponent into the air, you risk getting caught in the chokehold. To prevent such an outcome, it is important to ingrain the following fundamental steps into your brain. The first rule is to immediately establish control over your opponent's choking arm. The second rule is to circle in the opposite direction as you would when turning the corner for the takedown. The third rule is to dump your opponent to the mat but remain standing. If you go to the ground with him, there is a chance that he will maintain his hold. Lastly, keep your head up and your hips in. Following these rules will not only allow you to avoid the choke, but also finish with the takedown.

As I secure the double-leg on Ian, he attempts to secure a guillotine by wrapping his right arm around the back of my neck.

The moment Ian wraps his arm around my neck, I immediately take an angle by turning my body in a clockwise direction. As I do this, I pull his leg in between my legs with my left hand.

As I turn my body, I latch on to Ian's right wrist with my left hand.

Due to my previous actions, Ian falls to the mat. Notice how I remain on my feet—this is imperative. If you follow your opponent to the ground then you risk getting caught in the submission.

Having freed my head, I begin posturing up.

I step my right leg back, latch on to the back of Ian's right heel, and clear his legs.

I clear Ian's legs and pass his guard by stepping my right foot forward and planting it next to his right hip.

3.2: SINGLE-LEG FINISHES

DRIVE-THROUGH SINGLE

In the previous section I demonstrated how to finish the double-leg takedown by driving through your opponent. In this sequence, I demonstrate the same type of finish from the high single position. To be successful, you must control your opponent's hips, close off all space between your bodies, and pin his leg to your chest. When studying the photos, pay special attention to how I bury my head in my opponent's chest, almost as if I were trying to listen to his heartbeat. As long as you utilize proper form, you will secure a solid position and be able to take your opponent to the mat by simply driving forward.

I've secured the high single on Ian's left leg. Notice that I'm controlling his left hip and digging my head into his chest. With all space between our bodies closed off, his leg has essentially become a part of my chest.

Pushing off my left foot, I step my right foot forward, drive my head into Ian's chest, and pull his leg into my crotch.

I continue to drive into Ian by stepping my left foot forward.

Due to my forward pressure, Ian falls to the mat.

The moment Ian lands on his back, I step my left foot to the outside of his left leg and then circle my body around toward his left side. From here I will work my attacks from the cross-body position.

LIFT AND SWING FINISH

Having already covered the lift and swing finish from the double-leg, I will now show you how to perform the same finish from the single-leg position. As with the double-leg, you want to keep your head up and lift with your hips. Once you've hefted your opponent off the mat, swing his legs to the outside of your body to clear them and then drop him to the mat. Again, it is important to let your opponent hit the mat first. This gives you the option to drop down on top of him to cover and control him or remain standing and strike. As long as you keep your options open, you can make the best decision based on the present situation.

I've secured the high single on Ian's left leg. Notice that I'm controlling his left hip and digging my head into his chest. With all space between our bodies closed off, I've essentially made his leg a part of my chest.

Keeping Ian's left leg pinned to my body, I step my right foot behind his right foot, thrust my hips forward, and lift my head toward the ceiling.

Using the strength of my hips, I lift Ian off the mat and pull him onto my right shoulder.

Maintaining a strong grip on Ian's right leg with both of my hands, I swing his legs toward my left side by rotating my shoulders in a counterclockwise direction.

I drop Ian to the mat. From here I have a couple of options. I can follow him to the mat, cover, and control, or I can stay on my feet and throw hard strikes.

DUMP FINISH (CHANGING DIRECTIONS)

When I secure the high single position, I will usually execute either the drive-through single-leg finish or the lift and swing finish. However, I'll change directions and employ the dump finish if my opponent defends against both of those techniques by bouncing on his foot and sinking his hips back. To accomplish this, I immediately rotate my shoulder into my opponent's knee, take a couple of steps back, and dump him to the floor. If he should defend the dump finish, then I will immediately transition to the low single, covered later in the book, and work my takedowns from there.

I've secured the high single position on Ian's left leg.

I drive forward into Ian by stepping my right foot behind his left foot.

Before I can drive through Ian or lift him into the air, he turns to face me by rotating his body in a counterclockwise direction. As he does this, he escapes his leg and pushes my grip down to his knee. It's important to notice that I've maintained dominant head positioning.

Here I am doing several things at once. I drop my shoulder over Ian's knee and pull his leg toward my chest. At the same time, I step my right foot back and begin rotating my body in a clockwise direction. Notice that I've kept my head positioned underneath his chin while executing these movements.

As I continue with my previous movements, Ian falls toward the mat.

As Ian's back hits the mat, I catch his left foot with my left hand.

I clear Ian's legs by stepping my left foot back, circling around toward his left side, and throwing his left leg toward my left side with my left hand.

Maintaining control of Ian's left leg with my left hand, I step my left foot to his left hip. From here, I can throw some punches from the standing position or I can drop down on top of him and secure the cross-body position.

SECURING INSIDE LOW SINGLE CONTROL

When you secure the high single, the ideal scenario is to take your opponent down using one of the previous techniques. However, if your opponent manages to defend against those takedowns by forcing your grip down to his knee, you want to immediately transition to the dump finish, which was the previous technique. If he defends against the dump finish, then immediately secure the low single position using the technique below. In order to execute a smooth transition, you must slide your arm down to your opponent's ankle and elevate his leg above his waist the instant he forces your grip to his knee. This allows you to pull your head outside of striking range, as well as provides you with the leverage needed to execute the takedowns demonstrated on the coming pages. It is important to note that this technique also comes in handy when you shoot in for the high single but are unable to gain adequate control of your opponent's leg. Instead of abandoning your takedown, you change tactics by transitioning to the low single.

TECHNICAL NOTE: If you look closely at the photos, you'll notice that I have my opponent's left leg trapped between my legs. Due to this positioning, I will draw his leg up and across my body toward my left side. If he were to reposition his leg to the outside of my lead leg, which is quite common, I would draw his leg up to my right side. This alternate version will be demonstrated shortly.

I've captured Ian's left leg, but my grip is low on his knee, making it difficult for me to perform the high single takedowns previous covered. Instead of fighting for the high single, I will transition to the low single position by bringing his leg above my waist.

Keeping my right arm wrapped around the outside of Ian's left leg, I hook my left hand around the inside of his left ankle. It's important that you keep your head pinned to your opponent's chest to maintain dominant head positioning.

I cup my right hand over the top of my left hand.

In one fluid motion, I thrust my hips forward, pull Ian's leg above my waist, wrap my left arm around the back of his left ankle, and straighten my posture. It is important to notice that I still have my hands clasped together.

Keeping my posture straight, I position the inside of my left forearm underneath Ian's left ankle. To secure the low single position, I use my right hand to help pull my left arm upward. When done correctly, it will cause your opponent a significant amount of pain. From here, I will immediately execute an attack.

Having missed with the hook, I immediately cup my left hand around the back of Ian's left knee.

Using Ian's defensive position to my advantage, I crank his knee toward the mat by pulling down on his left leg using my left hand, pivot on my right foot, rotate my body in a counterclockwise direction, and step my left foot back. Unable to keep his balance, Ian rolls toward his belly and falls to his hands.

The moment Ian hits the mat, I release his left leg and prepare to secure top control.

3.3: BACK CONTROL FINISHES

DRIVE-THROUGH TO OUTSIDE TRIP

Earlier in the book I demonstrated how to execute the drive-through finish from both the double-leg and single-leg positions. In this sequence I show you how to execute the same technique from back control. To be successful with this technique, you want to drive your head into your opponent's back, pull his hips into your body using your bodylock, and then step a foot in front of your opponent's legs. As you drive into him, your leg acts as a barrier, causing him to trip to the mat. Just as with the other drive-through finishes, you'll be in an excellent position to secure top control.

I've circled around to Ian's back.

In order to secure a bodylock, I first need to form a solid grip around Ian's waist. I begin this process by crossing my right arm over the top of my left arm.

To secure a bodylock around Ian's waist, I hook my right hand over my left wrist and hook my left hand over my right wrist.

Having secured the bodylock, I step my right leg in front of Ian's right leg.

I press my head into Ian's back, suck his hips into my body, and push him toward my right side.

6

With my right leg serving as a barrier, Ian trips over my leg and falls toward the mat.

7

I release my lock on Ian's waist and throw him to the mat.

8

The moment Ian hits the mat, I latch on to his left arm with my right hand, push his arm across his body toward his left side, and place my left shin against his back.

LIFT AND DUMP FINISH (BODY SLAM)

In the seven basic skills section, I demonstrated the lift portion of this technique. Now I demonstrate how to use the lift to dump your opponent painfully to the mat. The technique works wonderfully when your opponent counters the drive-through to outside trip by stepping around your leg. Instead of fighting him, circle around to his opposite side and position your hips underneath his hips. Once you achieve this position, lift your opponent into the air using your hips, swing his legs to the outside of your body, and throw him to the mat. The movements should come very naturally if you've spent some time practicing the swing finishes I demonstrated from the double- and single-leg positions. There are other ways to set up this technique, but this is by far the easiest. It's referred to as the body slam because it gives you the leverage you need to throw your opponent to the mat with authority.

I've secured back control on Ian.

Having secured a bodylock, I step my right leg around the front of Ian's right leg, press my head into his back, suck his hips into my body, and push him toward my right side.

Ian blocks the outside trip by stepping his right leg around the front of my right leg.

The moment Ian steps his right foot to the mat, I circle around his left side, step my left foot in front of his left leg, and position my hips underneath his hips.

Keeping my arms wrapped tight around Ian's waist, I thrust my hips forward and start to lift his body off the mat.

6

I lift Ian into the air.

7

I throw Ian to the mat. From here I have a couple of options. I can follow him to the mat, cover, and control, or I can stay on my feet and throw strikes.

ROMAN CHAIR DROP

In the previous sequence you secured a dominant angle on your opponent and then performed the lift. Here you execute the lift while your body is square with your opponent's body. In order to be successful with this, you must secure a tight bodylock and position your hips underneath your opponent's hips. You must also explode your hips forward and use the power of your hips and legs to hoist your opponent upward. Once you've lifted him as high as you can, release your grip on his waist, hook your arms around the inside of his arms to assume the position known as the "Roman chair," and then slam him straight down on his spine. After impact, you'll be in a good position to either take his back or spin around to his side and secure the cross-body position.

I've secured control of Ian's back.

I step my left leg to the outside of Ian's left leg and square my hips with his hips. Notice that my back is straight and my hips are positioned underneath his hips.

I lift Ian into the air by driving my hips forward and arching back. As I lift him off the mat, I release my bodylock and hook both of my arms around the inside of his arms.

Sinking my hips back, I drop Ian to the mat.

I wrap my right arm around the front of Ian's chin. From here, I can work to secure the rear choke or circle around to his side and establish the cross-body position.

CRAB RIDE

Unlike the previous techniques in this section, the crab ride does not require you to lift your opponent into the air. Instead, you drop backward and pull your opponent down on top of you. In order for this to work to your advantage, it is important that you don't simply drop your butt to the mat and remain in a sitting position. You must use the momentum of your fall to roll to your back. This allows you to pull your opponent's feet off the mat and stretch his legs out using your legs, which gives you the room and positioning needed to secure back control and lock in the rear choke.

I've secured control of Ian's back. Notice that my hips are squared with his hips.

I release my bodylock, hook my arms around the inside of Ian's arms, and cup my wrists around the front of his shoulders.

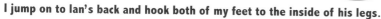

I jump on to Ian's back and hook both of my feet to the inside of his legs.

Having knocked Ian off balance with my previous actions, I roll to my back, pull him down with me, and extend my legs into the back of his legs.

Still extending my legs into the back of Ian's legs, I roll forward on to my butt and sit up.

As I sit up, I wrap my right arm around the front of Ian's chin. From here, I can work to finish him off with the rear choke.

PART FOUR: TAKEDOWN DEFENSE

OVERVIEW

Despite what many people think, wrestling is not based purely on scoring a takedown. Although it's a major part of what makes the art effective, takedown defense plays just as large a roll. This is why many wrestlers have been extremely dominant in mixed martial arts competition—they are versed in both arenas. If a wrestler feels his opponent has better stand-up skills, he has the ability to scoop him off his feet and take him to the mat. If he feels his stand-up skills are superior, he can utilize his takedown defense to keep the fight on the feet. And when I say "takedown defense," I am not simply referring to the sprawl. While developing an excellent sprawl will certainly make your takedown defense better, it is only one facet to the takedown defense game. In this section, you will learn how to thwart your opponent's takedown attempts using all your defensive lines, which include your hands, arms, chest, and hips. Not many MMA fighters possess this ability. Most skip these fundamental lines of defense and go straight to the sprawl, seriously limiting their ability to use their opponent's attack to their advantage. In addition to covering the lines of defense, I also demonstrate several methods for escaping the double- and single-leg takedowns should your opponent manage to penetrate past your defensive lines and secure control of your body. I strongly recommend spending an ample amount of time studying each technique in this section. When you become a master at takedowns and takedown de-

fense, you can steer the fight toward your strengths and your opponent's weaknesses.

TAKEDOWN DEFENSE 101 (p. 136-144)

When your opponent shoots in for a takedown, immediately resorting to the sprawl limits you to one defensive line. Instead, you want to employ all of your four defensive lines sequentially. First, attempt to stop the takedown using your hands. If your opponent gets past your hands, utilize your arms. If he penetrates past your arms, use your chest. And if you fail to block his takedown using your chest, resort to using your hips. It is best to think of each defensive line as a wall you're throwing up in front of your opponent. The more walls he has to break through, the harder it will be for him to reach your body. To help you down this path, I've included in this subsection the proper body positioning for each defensive line, as well as how to transition from one to the next until you stuff your opponent's takedown.

DOUBLE-LEG DEFENSE (p. 146-155)

If your opponent manages to penetrate past all four of your defensive lines and secure the double-leg takedown position, your first course of action should be to bump your hips forward into his body. This halts his forward penetration and creates an opportunity to execute the defensive techniques demonstrated in this subsection. If you fail to halt your opponent's forward momentum using the hip bump and he hauls you to

single-leg position. The reason for this is simple—the double-leg takedown attacks your entire body, while the single-leg takedown attacks only half of your body. In addition to it being much easier to mount a defense when only half your body is being attacked, there are also a lot more single-leg defenses to utilize. Honestly, I would have to say that 90 percent of my takedown defense focuses on warding off the single-leg, so it is extremely important to become a master at forcing your opponent into abandoning the double for the single. As you will see, this simple transition creates an opening to utilize the numerous escapes and reversals presented in this subsection.

the mat, you must resort to more extreme defensive measures. At the end of this subsection, I offer several methods for turning the tables on your opponent when he completes the double-leg takedown.

SINGLE-LEG DEFENSE (p. 158-172)

When my opponent penetrates past my defensive lines and secures the double-leg position, my primary method of defense is to force him to transition into the

4.1: TAKEDOWN DEFENSE 101

LINES OF DEFENSE

When your opponent shoots in, you have four lines of defense to stop his takedown—your hands, arms, chest, and hips. To utilize your first line of defense, all you have to do is put your hands on your opponent (sequence A). If he continues penetrating and gets past this first defensive line, then you want to position your elbows between your bodies (sequence B). If he manages to penetrate through your arms, your third line of defense is to drop your chest over his back (sequence C). If he gets past this barricade, your last defensive line is to sprawl your hips back (sequence D). Whether you are wrestling or fighting in MMA, it is important to always utilize these defenses sequentially. In MMA, rarely do you see this. The majority of the time a fighter will skip the first three defenses when his opponent shoots in and go straight to the sprawl. It's a poor tactic because it whittles his defense down to just one defensive line. If his opponent can get past it, the fighter will end up on his back. The only time I use a sprawl as my first line of defense is when I throw a big punch and my opponent ducks underneath it, allowing him to immediately penetrate past my hands, arms, and chest and into my hips. If you spend some time mastering not just the sprawl, but also the three defensive lines that come before it, you will not only increase your chances of blocking your opponent's shot, but also increase your chances of ending up in a position where you can remain offensive.

SEQUENCE A: FIRST LINE OF DEFENSE (HANDS)

I'm squared off with Ian. Both of us are searching for an opening to attack.

Ian drops his level and shoots in for a takedown. As he penetrates into my comfort zone, I place my hands on his shoulders.

SEQUENCE B: SECOND LINE OF DEFENSE (ARMS)

Ian has shot in for a takedown and penetrated through my first line of defense, which are my hands. Immediately I resort to my second line of defense by dropping my elbows and positioning my forearms in front of his shoulders.

SEQUENCE C: THIRD LINE OF DEFENSE (CHEST)

Ian has dropped his level and penetrated underneath my arms. Immediately I resort to my third line of defense by dropping my chest over his back, sinking my hips back, and placing my weight on top of him.

SEQUENCE D: FOURTH LINE OF DEFENSE (HIPS)

Ian has managed to penetrate through my first three lines of defense. As a last resort, I posture up and thrust my hips forward, halting his penetration.

FIRST LINE OF DEFENSE TO BASIC ZONE

In this sequence I demonstrate how to use your first line of defense to not only thwart your opponent's takedown, but also assume an attack position. As we covered in the previous sequence, the first step is to simply put your hands on your opponent. However, instead of trying to hold your opponent at bay, you pivot out of harms way and assume a dominant angle. Your opponent will most likely turn to eliminate your dominant angle, but before he can accomplish this, you launch an attack of your own. There are many different attacks you can utilize from this new position, and deciding which one to employ should be based upon your personal preference. In the sequence below, I demonstrate how to capitalize on your positioning by throwing a left cross.

I'm squared off with Ian in my fighting stance. Both of us are searching for an opening to attack.

Ian drops his level and shoots in for a takedown. As he penetrates into my comfort zone, I place my hands on his shoulders and intercept his attack.

Before Ian can get his offense going, I secure inside control by pummeling my arms to the inside of his arms.

Using my arms to create distance, I free my right leg by sinking my hips back and stepping my right leg back.

Keeping my arms positioned to the inside of Ian's arms, I step my right leg to the outside if his left leg.

I secure a dominant angle of attack by pivoting on my right foot, rotating my body in a counterclockwise direction, and sliding my left foot across the mat. From here, I can immediately get my offense going with an attack.

SPRAWL DEFENSE (OPTION 2)

This sequence begins the same as the last—you throw a punch, and your opponent ducks underneath it and shoots in for a single-leg takedown. However, instead of positioning his head to the inside of your body, he shoots in with his head positioned to the outside of your body. Unlike the last technique where you used your arms to create separation between your bodies, in this scenario you want to free your leg by sprawling it straight back. At the same time, drop your chest over your opponent's back and distribute all of your weight on the back of his shoulders. The instant you free your trapped leg, use your opponent's forward momentum to your advantage by snapping him down to the mat. Once accomplished, secure a dominant position by circling around to his side.

Ian is in a standard fighting stance, and I am in a southpaw fighting stance. Both of us are looking for an opening to attack.

As I throw a right jab at Ian's face, he drops his level and ducks underneath my punch.

Ian penetrates underneath my right arm and wraps his arms around my right leg. It's important to notice that his head is positioned to the outside of my body.

As Ian drives forward, I hook my right hand around his left armpit and my left hand around his right armpit.

I sprawl my right leg back, sink my hips, and drop my chest over the back of Ian's shoulders. With these actions, I place a tremendous amount of pressure and weight on his back and force him to fall to the mat. To avoid smacking his head on the ground, he releases his grip on my leg and plants his hands on the mat.

Using Ian's forward pressure to my advantage, I step my left leg back, drop down to my right knee, and pull him forward using both of my arms.

 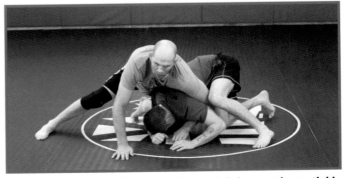

The instant I pull Ian to the mat, I circle around to his right side, rotate my body in a clockwise direction, slide my left knee underneath his right side, and wrap my left arm around his back.

4.2: DOUBLE-LEG DEFENSE

FORCING THE SINGLE-LEG

When your opponent shoots in for a double-leg takedown, he is attacking your entire body. If he manages to get in on your hips, defending against the takedown can be difficult to manage. However, when your opponent shoots in for a single-leg, he only attacks half of your body, making the takedown easier to defend. For this reason, anytime my opponent shoots in for a double-leg, I will try to force him into abandoning the double-leg for a single-leg using this technique. As you will see in the next section, this gives you a lot more defensive options. How much more? I would say 90 percent of my takedown defense techniques are for the single. So needless to say, when you are successful with this technique, you are in a much better position.

Ian and I are squared off in a standard fighting stance, searching for an opening to attack.

As I throw a right jab toward Ian's face, he drops his level and ducks underneath my punch.

Ian penetrates underneath my right arm and secures the double-leg.

DOUBLE-LEG CHOKE SLAM

This technique is very similar to the last—your opponent gets past your lines of defense, secures a double-leg takedown, and hauls you to the mat. You want to land on your far hip just as before, but instead of executing the hip heist and transitioning to front head control, you finish your opponent with the choke slam.

Ian has managed to duck underneath my right jab and penetrate into my comfort zone with the double-leg takedown.

Ian steps his left leg to the outside of my right leg and continues to drive forward. As he does this, I work to secure the choke slam by wrapping my right arm around his neck and my left arm over his right arm.

Ian continues to drive forward, taking me to the mat. As he does this, I twist my body in a clockwise direction, collapse my chest over his back, wrap my right arm around the left side of his neck, and hook my left arm over his right arm.

Having trapped Ian's head with my right arm, secured an overhook on his right arm using my left arm, and fallen onto my right side, the forward momentum from his shot forces his head to slam down into the mat. To capitalize on his stunned state, I hook my left foot to the inside of his right leg and elevate his body toward his left side. As I do this, I latch on to my right wrist with my left hand and then pull my right hand upward, driving the inside of my right wrist into his throat. It's important to note that I stay on my right side and pinch my elbows tight. To see how I position my arms, review sequence A.

SEQUENCE A: CHOKE SLAM AND HAND POSITIONING

To properly secure the choke slam, I wrap the web of my right hand around the outside of my left wrist. If I had my opponent's head trapped, this would drive the inside of my wrist just below my thumb upward into his throat. To finish the choke, I pinch my elbows tight to my body, push upward on my left hand, and rotate my left arm in a clockwise direction. These actions drive my left arm upward into my opponent's throat, forcing him to tap in submission.

BACK TO STANDING POSITION

In this scenario, your opponent executes a double-leg takedown and hauls you to the mat, but instead of landing on your far hip as you did in the previous two techniques, you land on your near hip and use your positioning to work back to your feet. The key to success is landing in the sit-up position and then instantly making your escape. If you land flat on your back or hesitate in the sit-up position, creating the space you need to escape to the standing position will be difficult if not impossible to manage.

Ian has managed to duck underneath my right jab and penetrate into my comfort zone with a double-leg takedown.

Ian steps his left leg to the outside of my right leg and continues to drive forward, sending me to the mat.

As I hit the mat, I land on my left hip in the sit-up position with my left hand posted on the mat.

In order to work back to my feet I first need to create distance. I accomplish this task by driving my right arm underneath Ian's chin, a technique commonly referred to as the cross face.

Having secured the cross face, I reach my right hand to Ian's right shoulder, elevate my elbow, and force his chin toward his right side.

Still driving my right arm into Ian's face, I use my left hand to keep my hips elevated off the mat, slide my left leg out from underneath my body, and plant my left foot on the mat.

I stand up and prepare to unleash an attack.

4.3: SINGLE-LEG DEFENSE

BASIC SINGLE-LEG ESCAPE

The technique demonstrated in the sequence below is a very simple way to defend against the high single. The primary objective is to secure wrist control on your opponent's inside arm and then slide his hand down to your knee. Not only does this create space, which drastically limits your opponent's options to attack, but it also makes it easy to break his grip and free your leg.

Ian has secured the high single position on my right leg.

In order to hinder Ian's offensive options, I need to create space between our bodies. I accomplish this by grabbing his right wrist with my left hand, wrapping my right arm over his left arm, picking my right leg off the mat, and then sinking my hips back and forcing his hands down to my knee.

I position my head to the inside of Ian's head. This prevents him from closing off the distance and reestablishing the high single.

To free my leg, I push down on Ian's right arm with my left hand, pull up on his left arm with my right arm, and sprawl my leg back.

CHEST WRAP COUNTER

Earlier in the book you learned that the proper way to establish the high single position is to close off all space between you and your opponent and plant your head on his chest as if you were trying to listen to his heart beat. When you're fighting an experienced wrestler, expect him to do the same thing to you when he secures the high single. If you are unable to create space and free your leg using the basic single-leg escape due to his tight positioning, your next best option is to force his head out of position by driving it toward the mat. Once you break his base in this fashion, you can either transition to front head control as demonstrated in the sequence below or transition to the choke slam, which is the next technique in this section.

Ian has secured the high single position.

I wrap my left hand around the back of Ian's head.

I pull Ian's head toward the mat with my left hand. With this action, I break his posture and dramatically limit his options to attack.

As I pull Ian's head down, I reposition my left palm against the back of his neck. Once I establish this grip, I push his head further down my body.

Having broken Ian's base with my previous actions, I rotate my body in a clockwise direction, position my chest over the back of his shoulders, and cup my left hand over his right shoulder. With his base broken, he struggles to maintain his grip on my leg and is forced to let go.

To keep Ian from reestablishing his grip on my lead leg, I sprawl my right leg back and pull him to the mat. From here, I have several options. I can attack from front head control; circle around his side to establish a dominant angle; or stand up, disengage, and set up an attack from the standing position.

THE ORIGINAL CHOKE SLAM

This is another technique that you can utilize when your opponent secures the high single. Just like the previous move, you begin by pushing your opponent's head toward the mat to break his base, but instead of transitioning to head control, you finish him by transitioning to the choke slam. The key to this technique is to bait him into abandoning the single-leg for a double-leg by stepping your rear leg forward and squaring your hips with his hips. As I mentioned earlier, double-leg takedowns are much harder to defend against. In an attempt to increase his odds at securing a takedown, he will most likely take the bait and reach for your far leg. The instant he does this, you have the space you need to get your rear arm around his head. To execute the choke slam, concede to your opponent's forward momentum and fall to your back. When done correctly, his head will slam into the mat. With your opponent dazed from the impact, maneuver yourself into position and finish him with the choke.

Ian has secured the high single position.

I place my left hand on the top of Ian's head and force it down my body and toward the mat.

Still applying the crank on Ian's right arm using my figure-four grip, I follow him to the mat and prepare to secure the cross-body position.

I plant my chest over Ian's chest to pin his back to the mat, drive my left knee into his left hip, and position my right knee next to his left shoulder. Now that I have secured the cross-body position, I will work to finish him off with the shoulder lock submission.

SINGLE-LEG DEFENSE

SHOULDER LOCK TOSS

Sometimes when you execute the shoulder lock foot prop to escape the high single, your opponent will step his hooked leg back to avoid the trip. When this happens, immediately counter his defense by transitioning to the shoulder lock toss demonstrated in the sequence below. There are several things that you must keep in mind when executing this maneuver. First, never break your figure-four grip on your opponent's arm because it will give him an opportunity to escape. Second, make your transition to the toss the instant he defends against the foot prop. Lastly, remember to hip heist over your opponent's body as you land on the mat. If you fail to execute these three requirements, you will not only lose the submission, but you will also compromise your position.

I've managed to secure a shoulder lock on Ian's right arm.

Ian steps his left leg back to avoid the shoulder lock foot prop.

The instant Ian steps his left leg back, I rotate my body in a counterclockwise direction and hook my right leg around the outside of his right leg.

DIRTY BOXING

Keeping my figure-four grip locked tight around Ian's right arm, I rotate my hips and shoulders in a counterclockwise direction, kick my right leg into the back of his right leg, and sweep him to the mat. It's important to note that this is one explosive movement. I am sweeping my leg back while twisting my body in the opposite direction. When my opponent falls to the mat, I follow him to the ground by planting my right shoulder on the right side of his head.

As we hit the floor, I drive my left foot off the mat and swing my hips over the top of Ian's body. It's important to use the momentum of the throw to execute this movement. It's not broken into steps as shown here. Steps three, four, and five should be done as one fluid movement.

Having swung my body over Ian's body, I land in the cross-body position on his left side. From here, I will work to finish him with the shoulder lock.

HIP TOSS COUNTER

When your opponent secures the high single, it can sometimes be difficult to pull his head down toward the mat to break his base. By the same token, it can also sometimes be hard to create space by forcing his grip down to your knee, especially when up against a wrestler with a strong base. If none of the techniques I've previously demonstrated work, the hip toss is an excellent countering option. When done properly, not only will you escape the single-leg, but you will also take your opponent to the mat and obtain top control.

Ian has secured the high single position on my right leg.

I hook my right arm around the back of Ian's left arm and grab his right elbow with my left hand.

I pull up on Ian's left arm with my right arm, pull down on his right arm with my left hand, twist my body in a counterclockwise direction, and hook my right leg around the inside of his left leg.

Still pulling up on Ian's left arm with my whizzer, pulling down on his right arm with my left hand, and twisting my body in a counterclockwise direction, I kick my right leg back into his left leg and drive my hips into his hips.

I hop my left foot to the inside of Ian's grounded right leg while continuing with my previous actions, causing Ian to plummet toward the mat.

As Ian lands on the mat, I step my right foot to the ground. From here, I can work some ground and pound, follow him to the mat and secure top control, or disengage and work my attacks from the standing position.

SINGLE-LEG DEFENSE

HIP TOSS TO CHEST WRAP COUNTER

Although the hip toss is an effective way to counter the high single, sometimes your opponent will defend against the throw by hopping on his grounded leg and stepping his opposite leg back. However, this positions his head over your hips, allowing you to capitalize on his defense by snapping his head down and securing front head control. It is important to note that in order for this technique to work, you must commit to the hip toss counter. Only if your opponent defends should you transition to the chest wrap technique. Like all secondary attacks, timing is your key to success. If you hesitate in the slightest, it is highly unlikely that you'll turn the tables in your favor.

Ian has secured the high single position on my right leg. In defense, I hook my right arm around the back of his left arm to form a whizzer grip and latch on to his right triceps with my left hand.

I pull up on Ian's left arm with my right arm, pull down on his right arm with my left hand, twist my body in a counterclockwise direction, and kick my right leg back into the inside of his left leg.

Ian defends the hip toss by hopping on his right foot and stepping his left leg back, clearing my right hook. The moment he does this, I plant my right foot to the mat and turn into him. It's important to notice how his head is positioned over his hips—this allows me to immediately transition to front head control.

To capitalize on Ian's current position, I cover the back of his shoulders with my chest and slide my left grip up the back of his right arm.

To prevent Ian from reestablishing his grip on my lead leg, I sprawl my right leg back and pull him to the mat.

I continue to pull Ian toward the mat by dropping my right knee. From here, I have several options. I can attack from front head control, circle around his side to establish a dominant angle, or disengage and set up an attack from the stand-up position.

PART FIVE: STRIKING

OVERVIEW

This section focuses on two quintessential strategies—striking your way into the clinch and reestablishing the clinch with strikes. In today's mixed martial arts competition, every competitor works tirelessly on defense, and this includes the clinch. If you step blindly toward your opponent to establish the clinch, chances are he is either going to counter with strikes or employ an evasive technique. By utilizing strikes to set up the clinch, you not only cause damage to your opponent, but you also distract him from your real intentions, making it much easier to transition into your desired realm of combat. However, it is important to realize that once you do manage to establish the clinch, your opponent won't let you do as you please. If he feels that you are dominant in the clinch, he will most likely employ a technique to disengage. Although he might be successful in his goal, he will be vulnerable to strikes as he backs away. Training to capitalize on this opportunity is a must. In addition to allowing you to cause your opponent damage, it also allows you to distract him and once again establish the clinch. The entire goal with this section is to learn how to blend your strikes and takedowns into fluid combinations to overwhelm your opponent and break down his defenses. If he chooses to defend against your strikes, he becomes vulnerable to the takedown. If he chooses to defend against your takedown, he becomes vulnerable to strikes. As long as you can transition seamlessly back and forth between the two, you will constantly be on the offensive. If you choose to ignore this important aspect of fighting, it will be very difficult to pull off a vast majority of the techniques demonstrated in this book.

5.1 STRIKING TO THE CLINCH (p. 176-184)

In order to successfully execute a double- or single-leg takedown, you must first get past your opponent's defensive lines. This can be extremely difficult to accomplish when you shoot blindly in from the outside. Unless your opponent has been living under a rock for the past ten years, he will most likely see the takedown coming, employ his defense, and put you in an awkward position that leaves you vulnerable to taking damage. A much better approach is to set up your single- and double-leg takedowns with strikes. In order to be effective, you can't throw a half-assed jab or cross. To steal your opponent's focus away from the

takedown, you must throw your strikes with the intent to do damage. When you throw a punch at your opponent's face with enough power to shatter his nose or open a cut, it generates a flinch response, which in turn allows you to duck underneath his defensive lines and secure a takedown position. Remember, MMA is not a boxing match where you can work your way into the pocket before beginning your delivery of punches. Due to the small gloves the combatants wear, such a tactic will usually get you knocked out right quick. You always want to throw your punches as you move into the pocket, and then continue forward so you can shoot in for a takedown or tie your opponent up in the clinch. If you manage to knock your opponent out as you move forward, it's all the better. But at the very least you will have closed the distance. To help you down the path of setting up your shots with strikes, I demonstrate several punch/takedown combinations, as well as several techniques that allow you to slip your opponent's strikes and counter with a shot.

5.2 REESTABLISHING THE CLINCH (p. 186-194)

When you manage to close the distance and tie your opponent up in the clinch, the goal is to immediately transition into a control position and set up a takedown or employ one of the techniques presented in the following chapter. The longer you can remain tied up with your opponent, the better your chances of causing him damage and securing a takedown. However, if your opponent realizes that you're dominant in the clinch, he will most likely attempt a quick escape and disengage. For a brief moment as he makes his getaway, his hands will most likely be down by his sides, making his head highly vulnerable to strikes. In this section, I demonstrate several ways to capitalize on that vulnerability. With each technique, it is important to throw your strikes with the intent to do damage. As long as you manage to threaten your opponent, he will usually elevate his hands to protect his face, removing his focus from his legs and allowing you to attack with a single- or double-leg takedown. It is important to note that range should dictate the combination that you utilize. If your opponent backs into punching

range as he disengages, throwing a hook or cross and then reattaching yourself to his body to tie him back up in the clinch is an excellent option. If he backs into kicking range, reestablishing the clinch is out of the question, making throwing a head kick your best bet. As I mentioned in the introduction, switching back and forth from wrestling mode to striking mode is an excellent way to throw off your opponent's defenses and create openings to attack.

5.1: STRIKING INTO THE CLINCH

STEP-IN JAB/CROSS TO DOUBLE-LEG

In this sequence, I demonstrate how to set up a double-leg takedown using a jab-to-cross combination. To be effective with this technique, there are a few things you must accomplish. For starters, you must throw the jab and the cross with the intent to do damage. When you threaten your opponent with your strikes, it forces him to bring his focus high, giving you an opportunity to drop your level and close the distance. Throwing lazy, half-assed punches only alerts your opponent to the fact that you're trying to set up another technique. Second, always step your lead foot into your opponent's comfort zone as you throw the jab. In addition to helping you close the distance, your forward momentum will add more power to your punch. If you throw the jab without stepping, you will most likely be out of range to land your follow-up strike, which is the cross (see example A). And if you're out of range to land the cross, your opponent won't be in any danger, making closing the distance difficult. Third, when you throw the cross, drop your level down into a crouched stance. This puts you in a perfect position to immediately follow up with a double-leg takedown. Finally, it is important to remember that your main goal is to close the distance into the clinch. Successfully completing the double-leg is great, but if your opponent should block the double, increase your elevation, tie him up in the clinch, and begin working for a takedown.

EXAMPLE A: OUT OF RANGE

I'm squared off with Ian in my fighting stance. Both of us are looking for an opening to attack.

I throw a right jab at Ian's head, but because I failed to step my lead leg forward as I threw the punch, I miss my strike, leaving me vulnerable to counterattacks. To see the proper way to throw the jab in this combination, see example B.

EXAMPLE B: STEPPING IN RANGE

I'm squared off with Ian in my fighting stance. Both of us are looking for an opening to attack.

Driving off my left foot, I step forward with my right foot, drop my level, and throw a powerful right jab to Ian's face. To protect myself from counterstrikes, I shrug my right shoulder above my chin and keep my left hand pinned to the left side of my face.

As I draw my right arm back into my stance, I rotate my hips and shoulders in a clockwise direction, drop my elevation, and throw a left cross at Ian's face. To protect my face against counterstrikes, I shrug my left shoulder above my chin and keep my right hand high.

Having stunned Ian with my strikes, I bring my right hand back into my stance and continue to penetrate forward. When shooting in for the double-leg, it's imperative that you keep both of your hands high to protect your face against knees.

I drive forward into Ian's comfort zone by shooting my head to outside of his left hip and wrapping both of my arms around the back of his legs. It's important to notice that my head is up and my back is straight.

Still driving forward, I step my left foot in between Ian's legs. From here, I can finish him with the drive-through double-leg finish. To see this technique, flip back to the section devoted to double-leg takedowns.

OVERHAND TO UNDERHOOK CONTROL

The overhand is another punch that I frequently use to close the distance into the clinch. As with the previous technique, there are several things to keep in mind when throwing this strike. The first and most important rule is to keep your lead hand glued to the side of your head. This protects you from getting caught with a head kick, knee, or wide hook. The second rule when throwing the overhand is to take an outward step with your lead foot and dip your head slightly. In addition to generating more power for the strike, this movement puts your head off to the side and protects you from getting hit by straight punches such as the jab and cross. Remember, even when launching attacks, you must be wary of your opponent's strikes. As long as you follow the two rules above, you will be protected from his straight punches as well as his circular punches. The last thing to remember is to not hesitate once you've landed your strike. The instant it connects, immediately tie your opponent up in the clinch as demonstrated below or shoot in for a takedown. Deciding which option to choose should be based on the openings created by your strike.

Ian is standing in a standard stance with his left foot forward and I am standing in a southpaw fighting stance with my right foot forward. Both of us are looking for an opening to attack.

I take a long step forward with my right foot and throw a heavy overhand left to Ian's chin. It's important to notice that I've stepped my right foot to the outside of his lead foot, creating a dominant angle of attack. In an attempt to land a counterstrike, he throws a left hook at my head. To protect my head against his counterattack, I keep my right hand high and block the punch using my arm.

Using the forward momentum of the overhand to my advantage, I step my left foot forward and close the distance into the clinch.

COUNTER JAB TO CLINCH (OPTION 1)

As you learned in the takedown defense portion of this book, you have four lines of defense for the takedown—your hands, elbows, chest, and hips. When you want to secure a takedown, you must get past your opponent's four defensive lines. The best way to accomplish this is to evade your opponent's strike by cutting an angle. While he is extended, his defensive lines will be down, giving you a brief window to capitalize on his positioning. To give you an example, I demonstrate in the sequence below how to evade your opponent's jab by slipping his punch using a side step, countering with a punch, and then capitalizing on his vulnerable positioning by closing the distance into the clinch.

Ian is standing in a standard stance with his left foot forward, and I'm standing in a southpaw fighting stance with my right foot forward. Both of us are looking for an opening to attack.

Before I can launch an attack, Ian throws a left jab at my head. As he extends his arm, I step my right foot to the outside of his left foot and shift my body toward my right side. With these movements, I move my head off-line from his strike.

As Ian's fist sails by my head, I rotate my hips and shoulders in a clockwise direction and throw a left cross at his chin.

Having countered Ian's left jab with a left cross, I close the distance into the clinch by stepping my left leg forward and to the inside of his left leg, sliding my left shoulder down his extended arm, and wrapping my arms around his body. From here I can work to take control of his back or execute a takedown from the clinch.

COUNTER JAB TO CLINCH (OPTION 2)

This technique is similar to the previous one in that I slip my opponent's jab and counter with a cross, but instead of closing the distance off the cross, I follow up with a lead uppercut. If you look at the photos below, you'll notice that when I throw the cross, I drop my elevation. This allows me to spring-load my body and throw a much harder uppercut. Once the uppercut lands, deciding what to do next should be based upon your opponent's reaction to your strikes. If he stands his ground, immediately closing the distance and tying him up in the clinch as demonstrated below is an excellent option. However, if he retreats backward from your strikes, throw another strike first and then try to attach yourself to his body. Range determines your course of action in any fight, so developing a keen sense of distance is a must. The best way to accomplish this is through drills.

Ian is standing in a standard stance with his left foot forward, and I'm standing in a southpaw fighting stance with my right foot forward. Both of us are looking for an opening to attack.

Before I can launch an attack, Ian throws a left jab at my head. As he extends his arm, I step my right foot to the outside of his left foot and shift my body toward my right side. With these movements, I put my head off-line from his strike.

As Ian's fist sails by my head, I rotate my hips and shoulders in a clockwise direction, drop my level by bending my knees, and throw a left cross at his chin.

As I pull my left arm back into my stance, I rotate my body in a counterclockwise direction and throw a right uppercut underneath Ian's extended left arm.

Continuing with my previous movements, I land a right uppercut to Ian's chin.

To capitalize on Ian's stunned state, I close the distance into the clinch by stepping my right leg behind his left leg, sliding my left leg forward, wrapping my right arm around his back, latching on to his left wrist with my left hand, and pinning my right ear to his chest. It's important to notice that I have his left arm trapped. From here I have several options—I can work for a takedown from my current position, circle around to take his back, or transition to two-on-one control.

STRIKING TO DOUBLE-LEG PENETRATION

In the previous sequence, I countered my opponent's jab with a cross, followed up with an uppercut, and then tied him up in the clinch. I throw the same combination in this sequence, but instead of closing the distance after landing with the uppercut, I throw another cross. Again, range determines whether to employ this combination or the previous one. If you are in tight with your opponent after connecting with the uppercut, immediately tie him up in the clinch or work for a takedown. If he is still within punching range, throw another cross and then use the punch to close the distance. The goal is to smother your opponent with your attack so he has no room to breathe. The more pressure you put on him with your strikes, the more successful you'll be at closing the distance and establishing the clinch.

Ian is standing in a standard stance with his left foot forward, and I'm standing in a southpaw fighting stance with my right foot forward. Both of us are looking for an opening to attack.

Before I can launch an attack, Ian throws a left jab at my head. To counter, I step my right foot to the outside of his left foot and shift my body toward my right side. At the same time, I rotate my hips and shoulders in a clockwise direction, drop my level by bending my knees, and throw a left cross at his chin.

As I pull my left arm back into my stance, I rotate my body in a counterclockwise direction and throw a right uppercut to Ian's chin.

I follow up the right uppercut with a left cross.

To capitalize on Ian's stunned state, I close the distance into the clinch by stepping my left foot forward, wrapping my arms around his body, and pinning my head to his chest. From here, I can work my offense from the clinch.

5.2: REESTABLISHING THE CLINCH

ELBOW (HOOK) TO UPPERCUT TO SPEAR DOUBLE

When a lot of fighters break away from the clinch, they have the bad habit of dropping their hands. If this should occur, an excellent option is to immediately throw a strike at his head. Again, the strike you choose to employ should be based upon range. For example, if he disengages but is still within clinching range, throwing an elbow is your best option (see caption 3A). If he backs away into punching range, a punch is usually the best strike to throw (see caption 3B). Once you capitalize on your opponent's mistake by landing a couple of hard strikes, you should be in a good position to reestablish the clinch or execute a takedown.

I'm tied up with Ian in the clinch. We are in a neutral position because we both have an overhook and underhook.

In an attempt to disengage from the clinch, Ian creates space between our bodies by stepping his right foot back. Notice how he keeps his hands down as he backs away. To capitalize on this, I will immediately throw a strike targeting his head.

I position my head on the left side of Ian's body and wrap my arms around the back of his knees.

To secure the double-leg, I step my left foot in between Ian's legs and drive my weight forward. From here, I can execute one of several double-leg takedowns. To see these techniques, flip to the section devoted to double-leg finishes.

UPPERCUT/CROSS TO CLINCH

In this sequence I demonstrate another combination that can be used to overwhelm your opponent when he breaks away from the clinch. It's similar to the previous combination in that I sock my opponent with an uppercut the instant he breaks away, but instead of following up with an elbow, I hammer him with a cross and then close the distance to immediately tie him back up in the clinch. Remember, if your goal is to take the fight to the mat, you must be relentless in your attack. If your opponent breaks away from the clinch before you can secure a takedown, damage him with strikes and then quickly reengage. The longer you allow him to remain on the outside, the better chance he will have of landing hard shots.

I'm tied up with Ian in the clinch. We are in a neutral position because we both have an overhook and underhook.

As Ian disengages from the clinch by stepping his right leg back, he drops his hands to his sides. Immediately I rotate my body in a clockwise direction and throw a right uppercut through his guard and toward his face.

Continuing with my previous actions, I land a right uppercut to Ian's chin.

Ian continues to disengage and backs away into punching range. As he does this, I rotate my body in a clockwise direction and throw a left cross to his chin.

As I land with the cross, I dive my left hand to the inside of Ian's right arm to secure a left underhook. To protect my face against counterstrikes, I keep my left shoulder shrugged above my chin and my right hand high.

I step my left foot forward to close the distance between our bodies and reestablish the clinch. From here, I can immediately get my offense going with an attack from the over-under position.

UPPERCUT TO HIGH KICK

In this scenario your opponent disengages from the clinch with his hands down, and just like in previous techniques you capitalize by throwing an uppercut to his chin. However, before you can use the uppercut to close the distance and reestablish the clinch, your opponent backs into kicking range. As you now know, range dictates the strikes that you throw, so instead of throwing a punch or elbow, you follow the uppercut with a kick aimed at his head. When you land clean, your opponent will often go down, but if he doesn't, you must quickly reset your base and return to your game plan—striking your way into the clinch and working for a takedown.

I'm tied up with Ian in the clinch. We are in a neutral position because we both have an overhook and underhook.

As Ian steps his right leg back and disengages from the clinch, his hands drop to his sides. Immediately I rotate my body in a counterclockwise direction and throw a right uppercut through his guard and toward his face.

your opponent locks on to your head, posture up, look toward the sky, and immediately transition to one of the techniques demonstrated.

6.1: OFF-BALANCING TECHNIQUES

INSIDE KNEE BUMP TO HEAD CONTROL

In this scenario, you and your opponent are tied up in the over-under position. In order to land hard strikes or haul your opponent to the mat, you must first off-balance him and secure a more dominant position. An excellent way to accomplish this is to employ the inside knee bump demonstrated below. When done correctly, the technique will put you into an excellent position to either throw a knee to your opponent's face or secure head control.

I'm tied up with Ian in the clinch. We are in a neutral position because we both have an overhook and underhook.

I drive my right knee into the inside of Ian's right leg.

As I drive my right knee into Ian's right leg, I push on his right shoulder with my left hand and pull down on his left lat muscle with my right hand.

Having pulled Ian off balance with my previous actions, I step my right leg back and wrap my right arm over the back of his head. To prevent your opponent from posturing up, it is important that you maintain downward pressure on his head using your left hand.

To secure head control, I cup my right hand under Ian's chin, wrap my left hand around the back of his head, and then drop my chest over the back of his head and neck. From here I have several options to attack. To see these attacks, flip back to the section devoted to head control finishes.

DOUBLE INSIDE KNEE BUMP TO HEAD CONTROL

Sometimes when you force your opponent's head down using the inside knee bump from the over-under position, he will regain his balance before you can land a strike or establish head control. In such a scenario, transitioning to the outside knee bump is an excellent option. It's the same technique as the inside knee bump, only now you're taking your opponent in the opposite direction. The key to success is to execute the outside knee bump while your opponent is still counterbalancing his weight from the inside knee bump because it allows you to use his energy against him. As he gets knocked off balance for a second time, it will be much harder for him to reestablish his base, making it easier for you to secure head control. Remember, the more you can keep your opponent guessing, the more success you will have at securing a control position, landing strikes, or executing a takedown.

I'm tied up with Ian in the clinch. We are in a neutral position because we both have an overhook and underhook.

To begin my attack, I drive my right knee into the inside of Ian's right leg, push on his right shoulder with my left hand, and pull down on his left lat muscle with my right hand.

I step my right foot back into its original position in my stance. This creates a hole for my opponent to fall into, which pulls him out of his stance and draws his head toward the mat.

Before I can secure head control, Ian postures up and maneuvers his body toward his right side to counterbalance his weight. To capitalize on this, I step my left foot forward and prepare to execute the inside knee bump on his left lead leg.

I drive my left knee into the inside of Ian's left leg, pull down on his right shoulder with my left hand, and push up on his left armpit with my right hand.

Continuing with my previous actions, Ian trips over my left leg and falls face first toward the mat. As he plants his right hand on the mat to keep from falling, I position my left hand over the back of his head.

With his body being thrown in a circular fashion toward the mat, Ian is forced to step his left leg back in order to regain his balance.

To secure head control, I cup my right hand under Ian's chin, wrap my left hand around the back of his head, and then drop my chest over the back of his head and neck. From here I have several options to attack. To see these attacks, revisit the section devoted to head control finishes.

INSIDE KNEE BUMP TO SHOULDER SHRUG TO ARM TRIANGLE

In this scenario, you execute an inside knee bump and your opponent counters by stepping his lead foot back, which puts the majority of his weight on your near shoulder. To create space and offset his base, immediately employ the shoulder shrug technique by snapping your shoulder into his face as though you were throwing a powerful punch or elbow. With his upper body forced away and his base disrupted, you have several options. You can work for a takedown from the clinch, execute a strike, or snag his head and apply the choke demonstrated in the sequence below. When examining the photos, pay special attention to how I control my opponent's head and set up the choke. It might seem like it's a difficult technique to pull off when first starting out, but after drilling it a few times, I think you'll find that it's a highly effective submission.

I'm tied up with Ian in the clinch. We are in a neutral position because we both have an overhook and underhook.

I execute an inside knee bump by driving my right knee into the inside of Ian's right knee and pulling down on his left lat muscle using my right hand.

Ian counters the inside knee bump by stepping his right foot back.

The moment Ian steps his right foot back to counter the inside knee bump, I rotate my body in counterclockwise direction and snap my right shoulder forward just as I would when throwing a powerful punch. Notice how my actions create space between our bodies.

Having created space between our bodies with my previous actions, I release my right underhook to begin setting up the arm triangle.

Utilizing the space I created, I wrap my right arm around the right side of Ian's head. Notice how I cup my right hand around the back of his neck. This will allow me to pull his head downward and begin setting up the arm triangle submission.

I pull Ian's head toward the mat with my right hand and secure head control.

With my right arm still hooked around Ian's neck, I immediately establish a figure-four lock by grabbing my left biceps with my right hand. When executing this transition, it is important that you keep your chest planted over your opponent's head to prevent him from posturing up and escaping your control.

To finish the arm triangle submission, I wrap my left arm over Ian's back and then pull my right arm up into his neck. At the same time, I use the weight of my body to force his head toward the mat. The combination of these actions restricts blood flow to his brain, forcing him to either tap or lose consciousness.

OUTSIDE KNEE BUMP TO HEAD CONTROL

While the inside knee bump is best utilized from the over-under clinch when you and your opponent have the same fighting stance, the outside knee bump is best employed when you are in opposite fighting stances. Executing the technique requires two simultaneous actions—bumping your lead knee into the inside of your opponent's lead knee, and pulling his upper body over your leg. The key to success is to perform both movements fluidly, and then get your body out of the way the instant you perform the bump. When done correctly, your opponent's head will fall to the mat, creating a perfect opportunity for you to land a knee strike or secure head control, as demonstrated in the sequence below.

I'm tied up with Ian in the clinch. We are in a neutral position because we both have an overhook and underhook. It's important to notice that Ian's right leg is back, which makes transitioning to the inside knee bump hard to manage. Due to this fact, I will immediately transition to the outside knee bump.

To begin my attack, I step my right foot to the inside of Ian's left leg and position my knee to the inside of his knee.

I flare my right knee outward and drive it into the inside of Ian's left leg. At the same time, I pull down on his right arm with my left hand and push on his left side with my right hand. Notice how these actions disrupt his balance.

I step my left leg back, pivot on my right foot, and turn my body in a counterclockwise direction. At the same time, I hook my right hand around the back of Ian's left shoulder and then use that grip to force his body toward my left side. Due to the fluidity of my actions, Ian falls face first toward the mat.

To secure head control, I spin around Ian's body and drop my chest over the back of his head. From here, I have several options to attack. To view these attacks, revisit the section devoted to head control techniques.

OUTSIDE TRIP TO TAKEDOWN

The outside trip is a highly effective off-balancing technique that can be used from the over-under clinch as a takedown or as a means to secure head or back control. As with most techniques, deciding which option to employ should be based upon your opponent's reaction to the technique. If he fails to defend against the outside trip, you will most likely be able to haul him all the way down to the mat and secure the cross-body position, which I demonstrate how to accomplish in the sequence below. However, if your opponent should defend against the trip by stepping his trapped leg behind him, you will want to counter his defense by utilizing one of the techniques demonstrated on the coming pages.

I'm tied up with Ian in the clinch. We are in a neutral position because we both have an overhook and underhook.

In one fluid motion, I step my left leg to the outside of Ian's right leg, wrap my left arm around the back of his head, and cup my left hand over his chin.

To upset Ian's base, I push on his left armpit with my right hand and pull his head toward my left side using my left hand. With my left leg serving as a barrier, Ian trips over it and begins falling toward the mat. It's important to notice how I use my grip on his chin to torque his head. This causes his whole body to turn, thereby throwing him off balance and allowing me to secure the takedown.

To counter the outside trip take-down, Ian steps his right leg back. The instant he does this, I hook my left wrist around the left side of his neck and apply downward pressure to his head using my left arm.

To avoid getting stuck in head control, Ian pulls his head away from my body. Instead of resisting his counter, I go with his movement by pushing his head toward my left side using my left hand. Notice how this exposes the left side of his body for attack.

As Ian postures, I drop my level, pin my head to his chest, and apply forward pressure by pushing off my rear foot. Notice how I've trapped his left arm between my neck and right shoulder.

OFF-BALANCING TECHNIQUES

Still driving my weight forward, I wrap my right arm around Ian's back and then hook my wrist around the right side of his waist.

I circle around to Ian's back by stepping my right leg behind his body.

To secure back control, I clasp my hands together so that my grip is positioned between Ian's ribs and hips. Next, I use my arms to pull him into my body, which causes him a considerable amount of discomfort. From here, I can immediately move forward with an attack from back control. To see the available takedowns from this position, revisit the section devoted to back control finishes.

DIRTY BOXING

6.2: DIRTY BOXING TECHNIQUES

INSIDE KNEE BUMP TO KNEE TO HEAD CONTROL

In previous sequences I demonstrated how to use off-balancing techniques to set up takedowns. In this sequence, I show how to use the inside knee bump to set up a powerful straight knee. Once you land with the strike, you can either follow up with more strikes or secure head control as demonstrated below.

I'm tied up with Ian in the clinch. We are in a neutral position because we both have an overhook and underhook.

I sweep my right leg across my body and drive my knee into the inside of Ian's right leg.

As I drive my right knee into Ian's right leg, I push on his right shoulder with my left hand and pull down on his left lat muscle with my right hand.

Having pulled Ian off balance with my previous actions, I step my right leg back and apply downward pressure to his body using my left arm. Notice how my actions create a hole for my opponent to fall into. As long as you time your movements correctly, your opponent will fall face first toward the mat, as Ian does here.

To capitalize on Ian's vulnerable positioning, I clasp my right hand around the back of his neck, use both of my grips to pull his head downward, and throw a right knee upward into his face. Due to the downward momentum of my pull and the upward momentum of my knee, my strike has devastating results.

Before Ian can regain his composure, I quickly secure head control by cupping my right hand underneath his chin and dropping my chest over the back of his head. From here, I can immediately implement an attack from head control.

INSIDE KNEE BUMP TO DOUBLE COLLAR TIE

In the previous sequence, I demonstrated how to off-balance your opponent from the over-under clinch using the inside knee bump, land a powerful knee to his face, and then transition to head control. It's an excellent technique, but a lot of times your opponent will pull his head upward after eating the knee to prevent you from securing head control. In such a situation, transitioning to double collar ties, and then using your control to keep him off balance and land more strikes, is an excellent option. Remember, you always want to pressure your opponent with a sequence of attacks. The more attacks you can string together in combination, the better chance you'll have of finishing the fight quickly and in devastating fashion.

I'm tied up with Ian in the clinch. We are in a neutral position because we both have an overhook and under-hook.

To disrupt Ian's base, I sweep my right leg across my body, drive my right knee into the inside of his right leg, push on his right shoulder using my left hand, and pull down on his left lat muscle using my right hand. Having been fluid with my movements, Ian falls toward his left side.

Having upset Ian's base with my previous actions, I step my right foot back and reposition my right arm across his neck. The former creates space and allows me to generate more power with a knee, and the latter prevents him from turning into me, grabbing my right leg, and hauling me to the mat.

I throw a right knee to Ian's face.

To avoid getting bashed with another knee, Ian postures up. As he does this, I turn my right palm toward the ceiling and prepare to secure a right collar tie.

I secure the double collar tie position by hooking my right hand around the left side of Ian's head and my left hand around the right side of his head. It's important to notice that I place my hands on his head rather than his neck. This supplies me with better leverage to drive his head toward the mat.

I pivot on my right foot, rotate my body in a counterclockwise direction, and step my left foot back. At the same time, I pull Ian's head down with my left hand and push his head toward my left using my right hand.

I throw a left knee to Ian's face.

INSIDE KNEE BUMP TO ELBOW TO UNDERHOOK CONTROL

In this scenario, you use an inside knee bump from the over-under clinch to upset your opponent's base and then execute a shoulder shrug to create separation between your bodies. This gives you a couple of options to attack. If your opponent is still within clinching rage after executing the shoulder shrug, your best option is to throw an elbow strike and then transition to underhook control as demonstrated in the sequence below. However, if your opponent gets knocked back into punching range from the shoulder shrug, your best option is to throw a hook and then transition to underhook control, which is demonstrated in the next sequence. With both techniques, it is important not to hesitate. Once you land your strike, immediately swim your arm to the inside of your opponent's arm. If there is any delay, you will most likely fail in locking in a dominant underhook.

I'm tied up with Ian in the clinch. We are in a neutral position because we both have an overhook and underhook.

To disrupt Ian's base, I sweep my right leg across my body, drive my right knee into the inside of his right leg, push on his right shoulder using my left hand, and pull down on his left lat muscle using my right hand. Fluid with my movements, Ian falls toward his left side.

With Ian now off balance, I rotate my body in a counter-clockwise direction and shrug my right shoulder into his head. Notice how my actions lift his head and cause him to fall backward.

Capitalizing on the space I created with the shoulder bump, I rotate my body in a clockwise direction and throw an over-the-top elbow to Ian's face.

I follow through with my left elbow and dive my left arm underneath Ian's right arm.

I secure underhook control in one fluid motion by stepping my left leg behind Ian's right leg, wrapping my left arm over the top of his right arm, and cupping my left wrist over his shoulder.

SHOULDER SHRUG TO HOOK TO UNDERHOOK CONTROL

This technique is applied in the same scenario as the last—you execute and inside knee bump to disrupt your opponent's base from the over-under clinch, utilize a shoulder shrug to create space between your bodies, land a powerful strike, and then quickly establish a dominant underhook. The only difference is that when you utilize the shoulder shrug, your opponent gets pushed back into punching range. Instead of hitting him with an elbow, you throw a hook. As I previously mentioned, the option you choose depends upon range. If your opponent is close, throw an elbow. If he is out of range for the elbow, throw the hook.

I'm tied up with Ian in the clinch. We are in a neutral position because we both have an overhook and underhook.

To create separation between our bodies, I throw my right shoulder forward into Ian's body. It's important to note that this is an explosive movement, much like snapping your fist at the end of a punch. At the same time, I clinch my left fist.

Instead of flattening my palm flush against my chest and pummeling my left arm to the inside of Ian's right arm to secure an underhook, I throw a left hook to his face.

Having stunned Ian with the left hook, I immediately dive my left arm underneath his right arm.

I wrap my left arm underneath Ian's right arm, cup my hand around his shoulder, and elevate my elbow. Notice how my actions trap his right arm between my left shoulder and neck.

I step my left foot behind Ian's right leg and circle my body around to his right side to create a dominant angle of attack. Having established underhook control, I have several options to attack. To see these options, revisit the section devoted to underhook techniques.

SHOULDER SHRUG TO COLLAR TIE TO STRIKING SEQUENCE

In this sequence I execute a shoulder bump from the over-under clinch to create separation between me and my opponent, but instead of using that space to immediately unleash a strike, I'll secure a collar tie with my overhook arm. If you look at the photos below, you'll notice that rather than wrapping my hand around my opponent's neck to secure the standard collar grip, I place my hand higher up on his head. Using this modified grip, I can pull my opponent's head down with ease, which in turn allows me to continuously disrupt his balance. As he struggles to regain his base, I land a series of hard strikes to his face using my free hand. The key to success with this technique is to constantly move and cut angles. You don't want to give your opponent any room to breathe. Just when he thinks he is about to reacquire his base, you switch your grip, pull him in a different direction, and continue landing punches to his face. When done properly, your opponent will feel like he is drowning.

I'm tied up with Ian in the clinch. We are in a neutral position because we both have an overhook and underhook.

To create separation between our bodies, I throw my right shoulder forward into Ian's body. It's important to note that this is an explosive movement, much like snapping your fist at the end of a punch.

Having created space with the shoulder shrug, I quickly secure a collar tie by wrapping my left hand around the right side of Ian's head. It's important to notice the exact positioning of my hand and arm—my hand is cupped around the back of his head, and my elbow is positioned in the center of his chest. The former allows me to pull his chin down to his chest, giving me control of his head, and the latter prevents him from closing the distance, wrapping his arms around my body, and securing a takedown.

I pull Ian's chin toward his chest using my collar tie.

Pivoting on my right foot, I rotate my body in a counter-clockwise direction, slide my left foot across the mat, and pull Ian's head down using my left collar tie. As I do this, I drop my right hand and prepare to throw a right uppercut to his face.

As I pull Ian off balance, I throw a right uppercut to his chin.

Still controlling Ian's head with my left collar tie, I cock my right arm back and throw a right hook toward the left side of his head.

I land a hard right hook to Ian's jaw.

As I land with the hook, I wrap my right hand around the left side of Ian's head to secure a right collar tie.

As I wrap my right arm around the left side of Ian's head to secure a right collar tie, I pivot on my right foot, rotate my body in a counterclockwise direction, and push his head toward the mat using my right arm. From here, I can continue to batter him with strikes from the dirty boxing clinch.

TWO-ON-ONE TO DOUBLE COLLAR TIE

If you read the section devoted to two-on-one control, you already know that your opponent's most common reaction to the position will be to step his lead leg back and switch his stance. Earlier I demonstrated a number of transitions and takedowns that you can execute based upon this defense, and here I show how to capitalize on your opponent's actions by securing the double collar tie position and landing hard knee strikes. However, it is important to remember that when you secure two-on-one control, your opponent will have a free hand to punch you with, making it critical that you initiate your attack the instant you secure the position.

I secure two-on-one control on Ian's right arm. Notice how I position my head in the pocket and pin his arm to my chest. From here, I will immediately move forward with my attack to prevent him from punching me with his free hand.

In an attempt to escape the two-on-one position, Ian steps his right leg back and creates separation between our bodies.

As I pull Ian's head toward the mat using my right hand, I throw a right knee to his face.

Continuing to drive Ian's head downward, I plant my right foot on the mat.

To capitalize on Ian's stunned state, I rotate my body in a counterclockwise direction and wrap my right arm around the back of his head.

DIRTY BOXING TECHNIQUES

I circle my body around to the front of Ian's head. To secure front head control, I collapse my chest over the back of his head, cup my right hand underneath his chin, and hook my left hand underneath his right armpit.

The moment I secure front head control, I pull Ian's head inward and throw a right knee to his exposed face.

6.3: TAKEDOWNS

SPEAR DOUBLE

There are a number of ways to set up the spear double takedown, but I find it works best from the double collar tie position. With your hands clasped behind your opponent's head and applying downward pressure, his natural reaction is to pull his head up and posture. Instead of resisting his upward pressure, you release your lock on his head, causing his body to jerk upright. As his torso straightens, you drop your elevation and shoot in for the spear double. When your timing is right, your opponent will have a very difficult time defending against the takedown.

I've managed to secure the double collar tie position and pull Ian's head toward the mat. The moment I pull his head down, he drives his hips in, pulls his head up, and works to straighten his posture.

Instead of resisting Ian's upward pressure, I release his head, causing his head pop up. To capitalize on his positioning, I immediately drop my elevation. To protect myself from potential counterstrikes, I keep both of my hands up.

With Ian's body postured, I drive my head into the center of his chest and wrap my hands around the back of his knees. It's important to notice that my back is straight and my head is up.

I step my left leg forward, drive my head into the center of Ian's chest, and pull his legs using my arms. The combination of my actions causes him to plummet toward the mat.

As Ian hits the mat, I position my hands over his knees. From here, I will either set up a pass or throw punches from the standing position.

INSIDE TRIP

To setup the inside trip from the over-under clinch, you must first generate a specific reaction out of your opponent. In this scenario, you and your opponent are both in a standard fighting stance, and you've secured a left overhook and a right underhook. From this position, you need to get your opponent to step his right foot forward, which can be accomplished by pulling down on his left lat muscle using your right hand and rotating your body in a clockwise direction. As he moves his right foot forward to counterbalance his weight, slide your back leg up to your lead heel (a movement I refer to as a cheat step) and sweep your lead leg around the inside of your opponent's lead leg. To get the takedown, sit your weight straight down to the mat. This last step is very important. If you allow your momentum to carry you forward instead of sitting straight down, your opponent can use your energy to his advantage by reversing the position and sweeping you to your back.

I'm tied up with Ian in the clinch. We are in a neutral position because we both have an overhook and underhook.

In order to effectively execute the inside leg trip, I first have to get Ian to step his rear leg forward. I accomplish this by leaning back and pulling on his right arm using my left hand. To maintain his balance, he will have to step his right foot forward.

As a result of my previous actions, Ian takes a hard step forward with his right foot to maintain his balance.

The moment Ian steps his right foot forward, I slide my right foot up to my left foot.

I weave my left leg around the inside of Ian's right leg.

I fall straight down to my knees, lean my weight toward my left side, and wrap my left arm around the outside of Ian's right leg. When executing this step it is very important that you fall straight down to the mat. If you allow your momentum to carry you forward, your opponent can use your energy to his advantage by reversing the position with a sweep.

Keeping my weight distributed over Ian's right leg, he falls straight to his back.

DRAG TO INSIDE TRIP VARIATION

As you learned in an earlier section, your opponent's most common defense when you secure the arm drag position is to pull his trapped arm back toward his body. This reaction makes him vulnerable to a number of highly effective takedowns, including the double-leg, single-leg, and the inside trip, which is covered in the sequence below. In order to be successful with the inside trip, the instant he pulls his arm back, weave your leg around the inside of his leg and sit your weight down over his hips. When done properly, your opponent will fall straight to the mat, allowing you to secure the top position.

I'm tied up with Ian in the clinch. We are in a neutral position because we both have an overhook and underhook.

In order to improve my position, I first have to clear Ian's right underhook. To begin this process, I lay my left palm flat against my chest and slide it to the inside of his right shoulder.

As I slide my left hand to the inside of Ian's right arm to clear his underhook, I secure the arm drag by bringing my right hand to the inside of his right arm until my thumb hits his armpit.

With my right hand, I pull Ian's right arm across my body toward my right side.

Ian defensively rips his right arm back and rotates his body in a clockwise direction in an attempt to face me.

As Ian turns to face me, I drop my level, weave my right leg around the inside of his right leg, wrap my left arm around the outside of his right leg, and hook my right arm around his left hip.

I collapse my weight over Ian's right leg and begin hauling him to the mat.

With my weight positioned over Ian's hips, he falls to his back. From here, I will immediately work to pass his guard and secure the cross-body position.

TAKEDOWNS

STEP-AROUND BODYLOCK

The step-around bodylock is another effective takedown that can be set up from the over-under clinch. To begin, you must secure a dominant angle of attack. If you have a left overhook and a right underhook, this can be achieved by stepping your left leg around the outside of your opponent's right leg and circling toward his underhook side. Ideally, you want to trap his underhook arm to the side of his body as you secure your bodylock because it will prevent him from posting his hand on the mat as you take him down. Managing this forces him to absorb the full impact of the fall and increases the damage that you cause. This is a very powerful slam when done correctly, but it is important not to get careless and fall back when executing the takedown. Instead, you want to sit straight down, just as you would in a chair.

I'm tied up with Ian in the clinch. We are in a neutral position because we both have an overhook and underhook.

Keeping my back straight and my head up, I drop my level, step my left leg around the outside of Ian's right leg, and wrap my left arm around his back. With these actions, I trap his right arm to the side of his body.

Having created a dominant angle with my previous actions, I secure a tight bodylock by clasping my hands together just slightly above Ian's hips on his left side.

DIRTY BOXING

Keeping my arms wrapped tight around Ian's waist, I thrust my hips forward into his left side and heft him off the mat. It's important to mention that the power from the lift comes from my hips and not my legs. If you lift with your legs, you will expend a considerable amount of energy.

As I lift Ian up, I corkscrew my body in a counterclockwise direction and throw him toward the mat.

As Ian crashes to the mat, I follow him to the ground and secure the cross-body position.

6.4: THROWS

BICEPS THROW

The biceps throw is essentially the same technique as the shoulder throw, a common wrestling move. Both can be set up from the over-under clinch, and both allow you to throw your opponent painfully to the mat. The only difference between the two is how they are set up. While the shoulder throw works extremely well in a wrestling match, it makes you vulnerable to choke holds. The biceps throw eliminates this vulnerability, making it a much more sound technique to use in MMA competition.

I'm tied up with Ian in the clinch. We are in a neutral position because we both have an overhook and under-hook.

Keeping a firm grip on Ian's right triceps using my left hand, I maneuver my right arm across his body and to the inside of his right arm.

I hook my right arm underneath Ian's right arm. Notice how I hook my right biceps around his right biceps. If you drape your opponent's arm over your shoulder instead, which is common with the shoulder throw in wrestling, you run the risk of getting choked.

Having pinned Ian's right arm to my chest using both of my clamps, I can now execute the back step. To begin, I rotate my body in a counterclockwise direction and slide my left foot behind my right foot.

As I turn my body in a counterclockwise direction, I pivot on both feet, drop my level by bending my knees, and slide my hips all the way through to the outside of Ian's hips. With this action, I pull his weight forward and load him onto my back.

Having pulled Ian onto my back, I drive my feet into the mat, straighten my legs, and heft him into the air.

As I lift Ian off the mat, I rotate my shoulders in a counterclockwise direction. Notice how I look in same direction in which I'm turning. This action ensures that you complete your rotation, thereby maximizing the velocity of the throw.

As I continue to twist, Ian catapults over my body and plummets toward the mat. Notice how I still have control over his right arm.

Ian slams down hard on the mat. From here, I can drop down on top of him and secure the cross-body position or work ground and pound from the standing position.

HIP THROW

As I mentioned in the introduction to this section, throws that incorporate the back step only work when your opponent is driving his weight into you. If you're tied up in the over-under position and your opponent is not feeding you forward energy, but you still want to utilize a throw that involves a back step, you must execute a movement that forces him to drive his weight forward. In the sequence below, I accomplish this by driving forward and pushing my opponent backward. Instead of letting me push him around the mat, he counters by driving his weight back into me. The instant I feel his resistance, I execute the back step and make my move. Although there are many throws that you can employ off the back step, I choose the hip throw in the sequence below because my opponent and I are wrapped up tight in the clinch. If there were space between us, I would have chosen the biceps throw demonstrated in the previous sequence.

I'm tied up with Ian in the clinch. We are in a neutral position because we both have an overhook and underhook.

Pushing off my rear foot, I press my weight forward and drive my right shoulder into Ian's chest.

Ian counters my previous forward energy by pushing back into me. Instead of resisting his pressure, I will use it to transition into the hip throw.

As Ian presses his weight forward, I rotate my body in a counterclockwise direction and slide my left foot behind my right foot.

As I rotate my body in a counterclockwise direction, I pivot on my right foot, grab Ian's right triceps with my left hand, and drive my right biceps upward into his left armpit. These actions force him to posture, which allows me to back my hips underneath his hips, close off all space between our bodies, and load him onto my back.

THROWS

Still rotating my body in a counterclockwise direction, I slide my hips through to the outside of Ian's hips. At the same time, I load him onto my back using my right underhook and by pulling on his right arm using my left hand.

Continuing with my previous action, I lift Ian off the mat.

Looking toward my left, I continue to corkscrew my body in a counterclockwise direction and pull Ian over the top of my back.

As I throw Ian over my back, I follow him down by dropping my right knee to the mat.

The moment Ian's back hits the mat, I slide my right leg underneath my left leg, drop all of my weight over his torso, and pin his shoulders to the mat. It's important to notice that I'm still using my left hand to keep his right arm pinned to my body. By lifting his shoulder off the mat in this manner, I can distribute more of my weight onto his chest and cause him a considerable amount of discomfort.

HEADLOCK TOSS

The best way to set up the headlock toss from the over-under clinch is to secure a collar tie and pull your opponent's head down. As you already know, your opponent's common reaction to the downward pressure will be to pull his head upright. The instant you feel his resistance, release control of his head and allow it to pop up. With your opponent postured, punch your biceps into the side of his head, step into his comfort zone, and chuck him through the air. The best part about this technique is that it gives you control of your opponent's head, which allows you to invert him entirely upside down during the throw and dump him square on his melon.

I'm tied up with Ian in the clinch. We are in a neutral position because we both have an overhook and underhook.

I bump my right shoulder into Ian's chest to create space between our bodies. Next, I use that space to wrap my right hand around the back of his head and secure a right collar tie.

I pull Ian's head down using my right hand.

Ian resists the downward pressure being placed on his head by attempting to posture up. Instead of fighting his reaction, I release my downward pressure, causing his head to pop upright.

As Ian's head pops up, I turn my body in a counterclockwise direction and slam my right biceps into the left side of his face.

6

Having knocked Ian off balance with my previous actions, I slide my left foot behind my right foot and back step into his comfort zone. It's important to note that I am keeping a firm grip on his right triceps using my left hand.

7

Still rotating my body in a counterclockwise direction, I slide my hips through to the right side of Ian's body. At the same time, I load him onto my back by driving my right arm into the left side of his head and pulling on his right arm with my left hand.

8

Continuing with my previous actions, I corkscrew my hips in a counterclockwise direction and pull Ian over my back. Notice how I am looking toward my left. This helps me commit to the throw.

I use the power generated by my hips to throw Ian over my back, drop to my right knee, and slam his head into the mat.

The moment Ian's back hits the mat, I slide my right leg underneath my left leg, drop all of my weight over his torso, and pin his shoulders to the mat. It's important to notice that I am still pinning his right arm to my body using my left hand. By lifting his shoulder off the mat in this manner I can distribute more of my weight onto his chest, causing him a considerable amount of discomfort.

6.5: DOUBLE COLLAR TIE DEFENSE
HIGH DIVE

When your opponent secures the double collar tie position, the high dive is an excellent technique to have in your arsenal. In addition to allowing you to escape a very vulnerable position, it also allows you to score a takedown. To begin the technique, drop your level, step deep between your opponent's legs, lift your head toward the sky, and shoot your hips forward. The combination of these movements accomplishes two very important things—it prevents your opponent from pulling your head down and landing a knee to your face, and it closes off all space between your bodies, which gives you access to his hips. To score the takedown, wrap your arms around your opponent's body, lift him into the air, and then slam him down to the mat. The key to success is to execute your shot the instant your opponent wraps his arms around your head. If you hesitate, he will sprawl his hips back, pull your head down, rip you off balance, and land knee strikes to your noggin.

Ian has secured the double collar tie position by wrapping both of his hands around the back of my head.

Before Ian can initiate his attack, I drop my level, step my left leg deep between his legs, and wrap my arms around his body. It's important to notice how I lift my head toward the ceiling, keep my back straight, and position my shoulders underneath his arms. The combination of these actions not only prevents him from pulling my head down and breaking my stance, but they also allow me to drop underneath his lines of defense and penetrate into his hips.

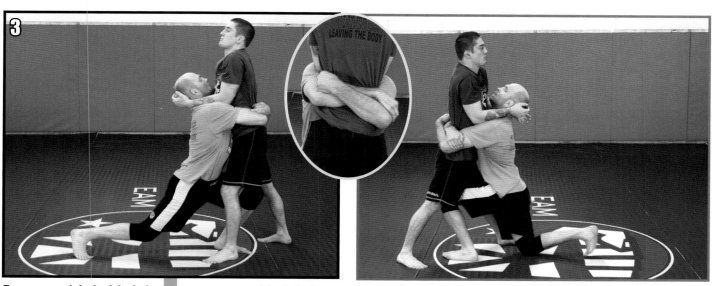

To secure a tight bodylock, I wrap my arms around Ian's body, cup my right hand over my left biceps, and cup my left hand over my right forearm.

Driving off the mat with my left foot, I thrust my hips forward and heft Ian off the mat.

As I lift Ian into the air, I slide my left foot back.

As I step my left foot back, I dip my right shoulder toward the mat and swing Ian's body toward my left side.

I slam Ian to the mat. From here, I can remain standing and work some ground and pound or drop to the mat, cover, and establish the cross-body pin.

CROSS FACE TO BACK CONTROL

When your opponent secures the double collar tie position, it can sometimes be difficult to shoot underneath his arms and into his hips using the high dive. This is especially true when up against an experienced Muay Thai practitioner who keeps his elbows pinned tight to your chest and his hips sprawled back. In such a situation, abandon the high dive and transition to either the cross face to back control demonstrated in the sequence below or one of the subsequent techniques. If you choose the cross face, the key is to cross-face hard enough to get your opponent's head to turn. This creates separation between your bodies and weakens his hold, allowing you to step your rear leg around the outside of his lead leg and secure a dominant angle of attack. As long as you keep your cross-face arm extended as you make this transition, your opponent will lose control of your head and expose his back, allowing you to secure back control and set up an attack.

Ian has secured a dominant clinch position by wrapping both of his hands around the back of my head.

Before Ian can launch an attack, I immediately create separation between our bodies by driving my left wrist into the right side of his face, a technique commonly referred to as the cross face. It is important to notice that I'm digging my wrist bone into the right side of his jaw. This causes him a considerable amount of pain and forces him to turn his head.

Still driving my left arm into the right side of Ian's face, I grab his left hip with my right hand, rotate my body in a clockwise direction, and step my left leg around the outside of his right leg.

Continuing with my previous actions, I plant my left foot on the mat behind Ian's left leg, shrug my left shoulder into my chin, straighten my left arm, and break his grip on my head.

Now that I have broken Ian's double collar-tie control, I can move to his back and secure a bodylock. I begin by maneuvering my left arm over the top of his head.

To secure back control, I wrap my left arm around Ian's left side, hook my right hand around the inside of my left forearm, and wrap my left hand around the outside of my right wrist.

STEP-AROUND TO HEAD CONTROL

When your opponent secures double collar-tie control, do not let him pull your head down. It shatters your base and makes you vulnerable to off-balancing techniques and brutal strikes. To avoid such an outcome, straighten your back and elevate your head upward as demonstrated in the second photo below. This gives you several options. If your opponent's grip is weak, execute a high dive and take him to the mat. If his grip is too strong to employ the high dive, you have a couple of choices. You can transition to his back utilizing the cross face technique, which was displayed in the previous sequence, or you can employ the step-around to head control transition demonstrated in the sequence below.

Ian has secured a dominant clinch position by wrapping both of his hands around the back of my head.

Before Ian can launch his attack, I drop my level, straighten my posture, and lift my head toward the ceiling.

Keeping my back straight and my head up, I turn my body in a clockwise direction and reach my left arm around the right side of Ian's head.

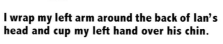

I wrap my left arm around the back of Ian's head and cup my left hand over his chin.

In one fluid motion, I step my left leg around the outside of Ian's right leg, shrug my left shoulder into my chin, posture up, and thrust my hips forward. Notice how these actions force his right arm off the top of my head.

With Ian's position compromised, he immediately steps his right leg back to create distance between our bodies.

Capitalizing on Ian's previous movement, I pull his head toward the mat using my left hand and work to secure control of his head.

To secure head control, I collapse my chest over the back of Ian's head and grab his chin with my right hand. From here I have several options to attack. To see these options, revisit the section devoted to head control techniques.

DOUBLE COLLAR TIE DEFENSE

TWO-ON-ONE TRANSITION

In the captions of the previous technique you learned that when your opponent secures double collar-tie control, turning your shoulder and applying inward pressure on his elbow weakens his grips. This technique utilizes a similar principle, but instead of reaching your left arm over your opponent's right collar tie as you did in the previous technique, you reach your left arm underneath his right arm and grab the triceps of his left arm. This gives you control of your opponent's arms, which not only allows you to use your free hand to rip his right collar tie off of your head, but also transition to two-on-one control.

Ian has secured control of my head with double collar ties.

I rotate my hips and shoulders in a clockwise direction, driving my left shoulder into Ian's right arm.

As I turn my body, I reach my left arm underneath Ian's arms and cup my left hand around his left triceps.

Keeping a firm grip on Ian's left triceps with my left hand, I grab his right wrist with my right hand.

I break Ian's control by rotating my shoulders in a clockwise direction, punching my left shoulder forward, pulling down on his left arm using my left hand, and ripping his right arm off the back of my head using my right hand.

Now that I have effectively broken Ian's control, I can transition to the two-on-one position. To begin, I pull his right arm into my right hip using my right hand and drive my left thumb into the crevice of his right armpit.

I cup my left hand around Ian's right biceps and step my left leg behind his right leg. To secure two-on-one control, I pin his right arm to my chest using both of my grips and place my head in the pocket. From here, I can immediately move forward with my attack. To see your available attacks from this position, revisit the section devoted to two-on-one techniques.

INSTRUCTIONAL BOOKS

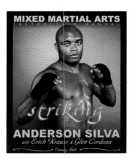

***MIXED MARTIAL ARTS
INSTRUCTION MANUAL***
ANDERSON SILVA

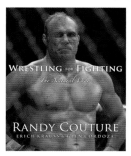

WRESTLING FOR FIGHTING
RANDY COUTURE

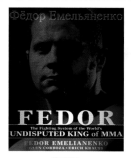

FEDOR
FEDOR
EMELIANENKO

MASTERING THE RUBBER GUARD
EDDIE BRAVO

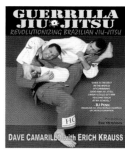

GUERRILLA JIU-JITSU
DAVE CAMARILLO

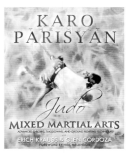

JUDO FOR MIXED MARTIAL ARTS
KARO PARISYAN

THE X-GUARD
MARCELO GARCIA

MASTERING THE TWISTER
EDDIE BRAVO

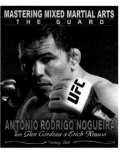

MASTERING MIXED MARTIAL ARTS
ANTONIO RODRIGO
NOGUEIRA

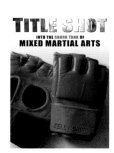

TITLE SHOT
KELLY CRIGGER

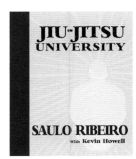

JIU-JITSU UNIVERSITY
SAULO RIBEIRO

***MACHIDA-DO KARATE FOR
MIXED MARTIAL ARTS***
LYOTO MACHIDA

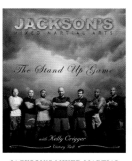

***JACKSON'S MIXED MARTIAL
ARTS: THE STAND UP GAME***
GREG JACKSON

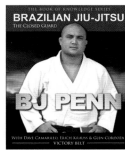

***BRAZILIAN JIU-JITSU
THE CLOSED GUARD***
BJ PENN

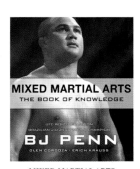

***MIXED MARTIAL ARTS
THE BOOK OF KNOWLEDGE***
BJ PENN

DVDs

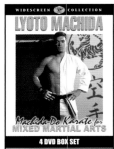

***MACHIDA-DO KARATE FOR
MIXED MARTIAL ARTS***
LYOTO MACHIDA

GUARD FOR MMA
ANTONIO RODRIGO
NOGUEIRA

***HALF, INSIDE HOOKS, &
DOWNED GUARD FOR MMA***
ANTONIO RODRIGO
NOGUEIRA

PASSING FOR MMA
ANTONIO RODRIGO
NOGUEIRA

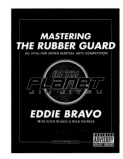

***MASTERING THE
RUBBER GUARD (DVD)***
EDDIE BRAVO

MATT LINDLAND, the 2000 Greco-Roman Wrestling Olympic Silver Medalist, is one of the top-ranked middleweight mixed martial arts fighters in the world. He lives in Oregon.

ERICH KRAUSS is a professional Muay Thai kickboxer. He has written for the New York Times and is the author of more than twenty five books.

GLEN CORDOZA is a professional Muay Thai kickboxer and mixed martial artist. He is the author of thirteen books on the martial arts.